PENGUIN BOOKS

THE POETRY OF BIRDS

Simon Armitage's *Selected Poems* appeared in 2001, and in 2007 he published a highly praised translation of *Sir Gawain and the Green Knight*. He has written two volumes of memoir about living in the North for Penguin: *All Points North* and *Gig*. He lives in Huddersfield.

Tim Dee is a BBC radio producer based in Bristol. He has written *The Running Sky* – a memoir of his birdwatching life.

The Poetry of Birds

Edited by
SIMON ARMITAGE
and TIM DEE

PENGUIN BOOKS

PENGUIN BOOKS

Published by the Penguin Group
Penguin Books Ltd, 80 Strand, London WC2R ORL, England
Penguin Group (USA) Inc., 375 Hudson Street, New York, New York 10014, USA
Penguin Group (Canada), 90 Eglinton Avenue East, Suite 700, Toronto, Ontario, Canada M4P 2Y3
(a division of Pearson Penguin Canada Inc.)
Penguin Ireland, 25 St Stephen's Green, Dublin 2, Ireland (a division of Penguin Books Ltd)
Penguin Group (Australia), 250 Camberwell Road, Camberwell,
Victoria 3124, Australia (a division of Pearson Australia Group Pty Ltd)
Penguin Books India Pvt Ltd, 11 Community Centre,
Panchsheel Park, New Delhi – 110 017, India
Penguin Group (NZ), 67 Apollo Drive, Rosedale, Auckland 0632, New Zealand
(a division of Pearson New Zealand Ltd)
Penguin Books (South Africa) (Pty) Ltd, 24 Sturdee Avenue,
Rosebank, Johannesburg 2196, South Africa

Penguin Books Ltd, Registered Offices: 80 Strand, London WC2R 0RL, England

www.penguin.com

First published by Viking 2009
Published in Penguin Books 2011

004

Selection copyright © Tim Dee and Simon Armitage, 2009
Foreword and Notes copyright © Tim Dee, 2009
Afterword copyright © Simon Armitage, 2009

The moral right of the editors has been asserted

For a list of permissions see page 335

Typeset by Rowland Phototypesetting Ltd, Bury St Edmunds, Suffolk
Printed in Great Britain by Clays Ltd, St Ives plc

A CIP catalogue record for this book is available from the British Library

ISBN: 978-0-141-02711-1

www.greenpenguin.co.uk

Contents

Foreword

Most of the poems in this book were written without the aid of binoculars. Who was the first poet to have them? Edward Thomas may have slung a rudimentary pair around his neck when he walked through southern England just before the First World War. Fifty years later it is possible to detect binocular-assisted poetry in some of Ted Hughes's work. Before our magnified century, John Clare managed to write about one hundred and forty-seven species of wild British birds without any technical kit whatsoever. He was exceptional (the greatest bird poet in the language), but his work reminds us that it is possible to get close to birds in all sorts of ways, despite living in a world ever-more mediated and increasingly depleted of species. Our commonest experiences of wild things are the birds we see all about us with our naked eyes. Usually the list is meagre and ordinary – a gang of high-stepping starlings crossing a garden lawn, two magpies twanging into bare winter trees, a quivering kestrel over a motorway – but once or twice a day perhaps birds like these (whether we identify them or not) catch our attention as they break from the backdrop. Poems are similarly adjacent to our lives. They are there, most of the time, at the edge of our vision or the corner of our mind, but once noticed they seem to gather brightness and potency.

I started bird-watching aged seven and became a hardcore field-man within a few weeks. Soon I was chasing rarities. It was a severe calling – pre-dawn starts, sojourns in sewage farms, monosyllabic companions, nights out in ladies toilets (dryer for sleeping) – and the idea of the poetry of birds, if I had ever thought of it then, would have been laughable. Seeing birds, and identifying them, was all that mattered. Anything else was just commentary and was for after the event, at best. It was quite a while before I read a bird poem. I got to know of John Clare's impressive tally from a bird book, not from his actual poems. But as I turned fifteen or so, I began to notice a few poems about birds that didn't taste off, that said things I could recognize, or even offered new observations that I hadn't picked up. One Christmas my parents, fed up with buying me stuffed birds or austere avifaunas, gave me *Crow*. I liked the thought that Ted Hughes had a pair of bins, and instead of submitting his reports to his local bird club had made them into poems. His crows weren't mine exactly, but I could see what he was getting at. And the real crows got more interesting as a result.

I began to read more. Nobody was saying very much out in the field, so in my mind I was able to run the bird poems I read up against the real thing. A sky with Shelley's skylark below Hopkins's and it below Isaac Rosenberg's; Keats's nightingale in a Hampstead thicket vying with Ivor Gurney's in Gloucestershire; Edward Thomas's blackbirds speaking to William Barnes's. From there it was a short step to imagining what those poets would have been like to be out with. Wordsworth walking ahead, able to see in the dark, and make it all reverberate; Coleridge, without adequate wet-weather wear and talking all the time, but animating the briefest of glimpses for hours after; Clare, quiet and private, and forever getting left behind, a tireless worker of his local patch, always wandering off and kneeling to nests; Hopkins rhapsodizing somewhat infuriatingly, but dazzling you with what he could actually see.

Not long after I read John Clare's description of a yellow-hammer's nest – 'Dead grass, horse hair and downy-headed bents/ Tied to dead thistles' – and when I discovered how similar it was to that in the masterpiece of British ornithology of the 1940s, *The Handbook of British Birds* (by H. F. Witherby, F. C. R. Jourdain, N. F. Ticehurst and B. W. Tucker) – 'Nest: Built of stalks, bents, and a little moss, lined horsehair and fine bents' – what had previously been separate enthusiasms flocked together.

The first bird-watchers who left descriptions of what they saw were poets. Homer's armies clash with the clangour of migrating cranes. The Anglo-Saxon poem, 'The Seafarer', includes bird notes written after a day among gannets on the Bass Rock. This poem and others of the very first made in Britain had birds in their sights, and almost every poet since has written bird poems. Indeed, it would be a challenge to find a poet who *hasn't* written one. True, not every poet has added bird species to county avifaunas as John Clare (sixty-five first descriptions for Northamptonshire) or Coleridge did (his nightingale in the *Lyrical Ballads* of 1798 gives us the earliest record of the bird in Somerset), but today's poets are no less observant.

If poetry and birds have coexisted over the centuries, poets and bird-watchers share another similarity. A declaration of interest in either, or (worse still) both, has prompted a certain awkwardness and embarrassment over the last one hundred years or so. Both have been thought weedy, romantic and somehow un-modern. There have always been bad – soppy, over-emblematic, under-observed – bird poems, and there still are. It is striking that although there were good bird poems written (with or without binoculars) between Edward Thomas and Ted Hughes, they tended to be rather chastened and oblique things. The birds in them were not as bright or as loud as they had been or were to become.

The term *subsong* describes the out-of-season warm-up singing that birds do; Kit Wright's poem captures it brilliantly. They sound like they are trying to cheer themselves through the winter. It has until recently been tempting to see much twentieth-century bird poetry as a subsong to past centuries. Not now. Things have changed and in the last fifteen years, there have been a remarkable number of excellent bird poems. Judging a prize in 2005, I read all of the poetry published in books that year in Britain. The single commonest subject was the blackbird. Poems about this thrush – many of them good – far outnumbered poems about war in the Middle East or any other apparently urgent topic. It was telling evidence that writing a poem about a bird is no longer a declaration of retrograde intentions or an abnegation of some higher poetic duty.

The challenge, though, is to say something new, especially since the airborne flock is already vast. The nightingale after Keats might be the hardest bird to write about, though an anthology of nightingale poems alone would tell a fascinating story about our relationship with the natural world over the past thousand years. Despite the wretched novelty of our dying biosphere, poems of species-extinction, ice-melt and habitat-loss are rarely other than vatic gestures. Close attention to the seen world and putting such looking into words remain as necessary as ever.

Once he had made nature legitimate again, for a time everyone went out with Ted Hughes's binoculars, and hawkish not mawkish poetry was de rigueur. Hughes's bird poems are brilliant juxta-positions of old nature, red in tooth and claw, written bloodily back into our new man-made world and what remains of the wild. Less disturbing, but no less original, poetry has dominated recent years. Birds are at the heart of some of the best new poetry in English by poets such as Michael Longley, Kathleen Jamie or Peter Reading (who regularly poetically name-checks his binoculars). Their poems can acknowledge great predecessors, they can articu-late the crisis of nature with great urgency, but they are also open-eyed meetings that are crammed with ornithological acuity and capture the direct experience of looking at birds today, giving us a comparable quickening to that which leaps up around any encounter we have with the real things.

There are roughly ten thousand species of birds in the world. Perhaps one thousand of these have been mentioned in poetry. Here we have gathered poems written in English on just one hundred species or so. There are more birds and many more poems, but we have concentrated on the poems we like most and which we think the best. These have included poems – and so birds – from North America, Africa and Australia. With so many to choose from we mostly favoured poems with real birds as their subjects. We wanted the air to be disturbed by wings or songs, not by a received idea; we wanted precipitation, not just climate.

The poems are arranged systematically according to taxonomy rather than chronologically or by poet. Ornithology is currently in a state of upheaval; extended studies on avian DNA are reconfiguring the great tree of world birds. Here we follow the order used in the monumental *Handbook of the Birds of the World*. This allows old and new poems about the same species or family of birds to sing alongside one another, giving a ghostly sense of generations of birds through the human centuries too (an idea already in Thomas Hardy's 'The Selfsame Song' and intimated in Edward Thomas's 'Adlestrop'). However, when gathering and making our selection it was also clear that there were many good bird poems that were not solely about a single species. To include these we have interrupted the systematic order with pages of poems about mythical birds, song, eggs and nests, bird deaths, and the largest and happiest category of all – poems that capture a day out watching what's about.

Tim Dee

Ostrich

He 'Digesteth Harde Yron'

Although the aepyornis
   or roc that lived in Madagascar and
the moa are extinct,
the camel-sparrow, linked
   with them in size – the large sparrow
Xenophon saw walking by a stream – was and is
a symbol of justice.

This bird watches his chicks with
   a maternal concentration – and he's
been mothering the eggs
at night six weeks – his legs
   their only weapon of defense.
He is swifter than a horse; he has a foot hard
as a hoof; the leopard

is not more suspicious. How
   could he, prized for plumes and eggs and young,
used even as a riding-beast, respect men
   hiding actor-like in ostrich skins, with the right hand
making the neck move as if alive
and from a bag the left hand strewing grain, that ostriches

might be decoyed and killed! Yes, this is he
whose plume was anciently
the plume of justice; he

whose comic duckling head on its
great neck revolves with compass-needle nervousness
when he stands guard,

    in S-like foragings as he is
preening the down on his leaden-skinned back.
The egg piously shown
as Leda's very own
    from which Castor and Pollux hatched,
was an ostrich-egg. And what could have been more fit
for the Chinese lawn it

    gazed on as a gift to an
    emperor who admired strange birds, than this
one, who builds his mud-made
nest in dust yet will wade
    in lake or sea till only the head shows.

        ★   ★   ★

    Six hundred ostrich-brains served
    at one banquet, the ostrich-plume-tipped tent
and desert spear, jewel-
gorgeous ugly egg-shell
    goblets, eight pairs of ostriches
in harness, dramatize a meaning
always missed by the externalist.

    The power of the visible
    is the invisible, as even where
no tree of freedom grows,
so-called brute courage knows.
    Heroism is exhausting, yet
it contradicts a greed that did not wisely spare
the harmless solitaire

or great auk in its grandeur;
   unsolicitude having swallowed up
all giant birds but an alert gargantuan
   little-winged, magnificently speedy running-bird.
This one remaining rebel
is the sparrow-camel.

                                        Marianne Moore

Emperor Penguin

On the Death of an
Emperor Penguin in Regent's Park

A proletarian, unlikely bird, no monarch,
Whose northern relation, the Gare-fowl or Great Auk,
One hundred years has been extinct on these islands;
An ugly, blubber-jacketed, wingless giant
Laboriously transported from his desert of ice,
His house of hurricanes (uncomfortable birthplace!
Cold and insanitary, where ocean hardens!)
Has perished in the Zoological Gardens.
Tell, masochistic martyr, what ailed you?
Here there is care and comfort; what can have killed you?
Speak, shade! Were your keepers neglecting your welfare?
Did you lack anything purchasable with silver?
O stupid, ungrateful bird! Blubber and feather!
To die of desire for freedom and bad weather,
For the perch where you, pegged to a glacier's bitter stone
Outlast an Antarctic unending cyclone,
And watch, neither superb nor able, from below
A smashed world whirl away in stinging snow.

David Wright

Albatross

The Albatross

Often, for pastime, mariners will ensnare
The albatross, that vast sea-bird who sweeps
On high companionable pinion where
Their vessel glides upon the bitter deeps.

Torn from his native space, this captive king
Flounders upon the deck in stricken pride,
And pitiably lets his great white wing
Drag like a heavy paddle at his side.

This rider of winds, how awkward he is, and weak!
How droll he seems, who was all grace of late!
A sailor pokes a pipestem into his beak;
Another, hobbling, mocks his trammeled gait.

The Poet is like this monarch of the clouds,
Familiar of storms, of stars, and of all high things;
Exiled on earth amidst its hooting crowds,
He cannot walk, borne down by giant wings.

Charles Baudelaire
(*translated from the French by Richard Wilbur*)

from The Rime of the Ancient Mariner

An ancient Mariner
meeteth three Gallants
bidden to a wedding-
feast, and detaineth one.

It is an ancient Mariner,
And he stoppeth one of three.
'By thy long grey beard and glittering eye,
Now wherefore stopp'st thou me?

The Bridegroom's doors are opened wide,
And I am next of kin;
The guests are met, the feast is set:
May'st hear the merry din.'

He holds him with his skinny hand,
'There was a ship,' quoth he.
'Hold off! unhand me, grey-beard loon!'
Eftsoons his hand dropt he.

The Wedding Guest is
spellbound by the eye of
the old sea-faring man,
and constrained to hear
his tale.

He holds him with his glittering eye –
The Wedding-Guest stood still,
And listens like a three years' child:
The Mariner hath his will.

The Wedding-Guest sat on a stone:
He cannot choose but hear;
And thus spake on that ancient man,
The bright-eyed Mariner.

'The ship was cheered, the harbour cleared,
Merrily did we drop
Below the kirk, below the hill,
Below the lighthouse top.

The Mariner tells how
the ship sailed southward
with a good wind and
fair weather, till it
reached the line.

The Sun came up upon the left,
Out of the sea came he!
And he shone bright, and on the right
Went down into the sea.

Higher and higher every day,
Till over the mast at noon –
The Wedding-Guest here beat his breast,
For he heard the loud bassoon.

The Wedding Guest
heareth the bridal music;
but the Mariner
continueth his tale.

The bride hath paced into the hall,
Red as a rose is she;
Nodding their heads before her goes
The merry minstrelsy.

The Wedding-Guest he beat his breast,
Yet he cannot choose but hear;
And thus spake on that ancient man,
The bright-eyed Mariner.

The ship drawn by a
storm toward the south
pole.

'And now the STORM-BLAST came, and he
Was tyrannous and strong:
He struck with his o'ertaking wings,
And chased us south along.

With sloping masts and dipping prow,
As who pursued with yell and blow
Still treads the shadow of his foe,
And forward bends his head,
The ship drove fast, loud roared the blast,
And southward aye we fled.

And now there came both mist and snow,
And it grew wondrous cold:
And ice, mast-high, came floating by,
As green as emerald.

The land of ice, and of
fearful sounds where no
living thing was to be
seen.

And through the drifts the snowy clifts
Did send a dismal sheen:
Nor shapes of men nor beasts we ken –
The ice was all between.

The ice was here, the ice was there,
The ice was all around:
It cracked and growled, and roared and
howled,
Like noises in a swound!

At length did cross an Albatross,
Thorough the fog it came;
As if it had been a Christian soul,
We hailed it in God's name.

It ate the food it ne'er had eat,
And round and round it flew.
The ice did split with a thunder-fit;
The helmsman steered us through!

And a good south wind sprung up behind;
The Albatross did follow,
And every day, for food or play,
Came to the mariner's hollo!

In mist or cloud, on mast or shroud,
It perched for vespers nine;
Whiles all the night, through fog-smoke white,
Glimmered the white Moon-shine.'

'God save thee, ancient Mariner!
From the fiends, that plague thee thus! –
Why look'st thou so?' – With my cross-bow
I shot the ALBATROSS.

Samuel Taylor Coleridge

8

Gannet

Rhu Mor

Gannets fall like the heads of tridents,
bombarding the green silk water
off Rhu Mor. A salt seabeast of a timber
pushes its long snout
up on the sand, where a seal,
struggling in the straitjacket of its own skin,
violently shuffles towards the frayed wave,
the spinning sandgrains, the
caves of green.

I sit in the dunes – the wind
has moulded the sand in pastry frills
and cornices: flights of grass
are stuck in it – their smooth shafts shiver
with trickling drops of light.

Space opens and from the heart of the matter
sheds a descending grace that makes,
for a moment, that naked thing, being,
a thing to understand.

I look out from it
at the grave and simple elements
gathered round a barrage of gannets
whose detonations
explode the green into white.

Norman MacCaig

Candlebird*

after Abbas Ibn Al-Ahnaf, c. 750

If, tonight, she scorns me for my song,
You may be sure of this: within the year
Another man will say this verse to her
And she will yield to him for its sad sweetness.

'*"Then I am like the candlebird,"*' he'll continue,
After explaining what a candlebird is,
'*"Whose lifeless eyes see nothing and see all,*
Lighting their small room with my burning tongue;

His shadow rears above hers on the wall
As hour by hour, I pass into the air."
Take my hand. Now tell me: flesh or tallow?
Which I am tonight, I leave to you.'

So take my hand and tell me, flesh or tallow.
Which man I am tonight I leave to you.

Don Paterson

* Generic name for several species of seabird, the flesh of which is so
saturated in oil the whole bird can be threaded with a wick and burnt entire.

A Day Out 1

from The Parliament of Fowls

Whan I was come ayeyn into the place
That I of spak, that was so sote and grene,
Forth welk I tho myselven to solace.
Tho was I war wher that ther sat a queene
That, as of lyght the somer sonne shene
Passeth the sterre, right so over mesure
She fayrer was than any creature.

And in a launde, upon an hil of floures,
Was set this noble goddesse Nature.
Of braunches were here halles and here boures
Iwrought after here cast and here mesure;
Ne there nas foul that cometh of engendrure
That they ne were prest in here presence,
To take hire dom and yeve hire audyence.

For this was on seynt Valentynes day,
Whan every foul cometh there to chese his make,
Of every kynde that men thynke may,
And that so huge a noyse gan they make
That erthe, and eyr, and tre, and every lake

sote sweet; *welk* walked; *sterre* stars; *over mesure* beyond measure; *launde* glade;
here her; *cast* design; *foul* bird; *engendrure* procreation; *prest* eagerly ready; *take
hire dom* receive her decision; *audyence* hearing; *chese his make* choose its mate

So ful was, that unethe was there space
For me to stonde, so ful was al the place.

And right as Aleyn, in the Pleynt of Kynde,
Devyseth Nature of aray and face,
In swich aray men myghte hire there fynde.
This noble emperesse, ful of grace,
Bad every foul to take his owne place,
As they were woned alwey fro yer to yeere,
Seynt Valentynes day, to stonden theere.

That is to seyn, the foules of ravyne
Weere hyest set, and thanne the foules smale
That eten, as hem Nature wolde enclyne,
As worm or thyng of which I telle no tale;
And water-foul sat lowest in the dale;
But foul that lyveth by sed sat on the grene,
And that so fele that wonder was to sene.

There myghte men the royal egle fynde,
That with his sharpe lok perseth the sonne,
And othere egles of a lowere kynde,
Of whiche that clerkes wel devyse conne.
Ther was the tiraunt with his fetheres donne
And grey, I mene the goshauk, that doth pyne
To bryddes for his outrageous ravyne.

The gentyl faucoun, that with his feet distrayneth
The kynges hand; the hardy sperhauk eke,
The quayles foo; the merlioun, that payneth

---

unethe hardly; *Devyseth* describes; *woned* accustomed; *foules of ravyne* birds of
prey; *sed* seed; *so fele* so many; *perseth* pierces; *clerkes* scholars; *devyse conne*
know how to describe; *tiraunt* tyrant; *donne* dun, dull-brown; *doth pyne*
causes suffering; *ravyne* rapine; *distrayneth* grasps; *sperhauk* sparrow-hawk;
quayles foo quail's foe; *merlioun* merlin

Hymself ful ofte the larke for to seke;
There was the douve with hire yën meke;
The jelous swan, ayens his deth that syngeth;
The oule ek, that of deth the bode bryngeth;

The crane, the geaunt, with his trompes soun;
The thef, the chough; and ek the janglynge pye;
The skornynge jay; the eles fo, heroun;
The false lapwynge, ful of trecherye;
The stare, that the conseyl can bewrye;
The tame ruddok, and the coward kyte;
The kok, that orloge is of thorpes lyte;

The sparwe, Venus sone; the nyghtyngale,
That clepeth forth the grene leves newe;
The swalwe, mortherere of the foules smale
That maken hony of floures freshe of hewe;
The wedded turtil, with hire herte trewe;
The pekok, with his aungels fetheres bryghte;
The fesaunt, skornere of the cok by nyghte;

The waker goos; the cukkow ever unkynde;
The popynjay, ful of delicasye;
The drake, stroyere of his owene kynde;
The stork, the wrekere of avouterye;
The hote cormeraunt of glotenye;
The raven wys; the crowe with vois of care;
The throstil old; the frosty feldefare.

---

yën meke meek eyes; *ayens* in anticipation of; *ek* also; *bode* omen; *geaunt* giant;
thef thief; *janglynge pye* chattering magpie; *eles fo* eel's foe; *stare* starling; *bewrye*
betray; *ruddok* robin; *orloge* timepiece; *thorpes lyte* small villages; *Venus sone*
son of Venus; *clepeth* calls; *swalwe* swallow; *mortherere of the foules smale*
murderer of bees; *turtil* turtle dove; *fesaunt* pheasant; *waker* watchful; *unkynde*
unnatural; *popynjay* parrot; *stroyere* destroyer; *wrekere* punisher; *avouterye*
adultery; *wys* wise; *throstil* thrush; *frosty* white-chested

What shulde I seyn? Of foules every kynde
That in this world han fetheres and stature
Men myghten in that place assembled fynde
Byfore the noble goddesse of Nature,
And everich of hem dide his besy cure
Benygnely to chese or for to take,
By hire acord, his formel or his make.

Now welcome, somer, with thy sonne softe,
That hast this wintres wedres overshake,
And driven away the longe nyghtes blake!

Saynt Valentyn, that art ful hy on-lofte,
Thus syngen smale foules for thy sake:
Now welcome, somer, with thy sonne softe,
That hast this wintres wedres overshake.

Geoffrey Chaucer

From Philip Sparrow

Lauda, anima mea, Dominum!
To weep with me look that ye come
All manner of birdes in your kind;
See none be left behind.
To mourning looke that ye fall
With dolorous songes funeral,
Some to sing, and some to say,
Some to weep, and some to pray,
Every bird in his lay.

dide his besy cure worked diligently; *benygnely* graciously; *chese* choose; *formel*
female (bird); *make* mate; *sonne* sun; *wedres overshake* storms shaken off; *on-lofte*
on high

The goldfinch, the wagtail;
The jangling jay to rail,
The flecked pie to chatter
Of this dolorous matter;
And robin redbreast,
He shall be the priest
The requiem mass to sing,
Softly warbeling,
With help of the reed sparrow,
And the chatteringe swallow,
This hearse for to hallow;
The lark with his long toe;
The spink and the martinet also;
The shoveller with his broad beak;
The dotterel, that foolish peke,
And also the mad coot,
With balde face to toot;
The fieldfare and the snite;
The crow and the kite;
The raven, called Rolfe,
His plain-song to sol-fa;
The partridge, the quail;
The plover with us to wail;
The woodhack that singeth 'chur'
Hoarsely, as he had the mur;
The lusty chanting nightingale;
The popinjay to tell her tale,
That toteth oft in a glass,
Shall read the Gospel at mass;
The mavis with her whistle
Shall read there the Epistle.
But with a large and a long
To keep just plain-song,
Our chanters shall be the cuckoo,
The culver, the stockdowe,
With 'peewit' the lapwing

The versicles shall sing.
The bittern with his bumpe,
The crane with his trumpe,
The swan of Maeander,
The goose and the gander,
The duck and the drake,
Shall watch at this wake;
The peacock so proud,
Because his voice is loud,
And hath a glorious tail,
He shall sing the Grail;
The owl, that is so foul,
Must help us to howl;
The heron so gaunt,
And the cormorant,
With the pheasant,
And the gaggling gant,
And the churlish chough;
The knot and the ruff;
The barnacle, the buzzard,
With the mild mallard;
The divendop to sleep;
The water-hen to weep;
The puffin and the teal
Money they shall deal
To poore folk at large,
That shall be their charge,
The seamew and the titmouse;
The woodcock with the longe nose
The throstle with her warbling;
The starling with her brabling;
The rook with the osprey
That putteth fishes to a fray;
And the dainty curlew,
With turtle most true.
At this Placebo

We may not well forgo
The countering of the coe;
The stork also,
That maketh his nest
In chimneys to rest;
Within those walls
No broken galls
May there abide
Of cuckoldry side,
Or else philosophy
Maketh a great lie.
The Ostrich that will eat
An horseshoe so great,
In the stead of meat,
Such fervent heat
His stomach cloth frete;
He cannot well fly,
Not sing tunably,
Yet at a brayd
He hath well assayed
To sol-fa above E-la.
Fa, lorell, *fa, fa*!
Ne quando
Male cantando.
The best that ever we can,
To make him our bell-man,
And let him ring the bells.
He can do nothing else

[. . .]

But for the eagle doth fly
Highest in the sky,
He shall be the sub-dean,
The choir to demean,
As provost principal,

17

To teach them their Ordinal;
Also the noble falcon,
With the ger-falcon,
The tarsil gentil,
They shall mourn soft and still
In their amice of grey;
The saker with them shall say
Dirige for Philip's soul;
The goshawk shall have a role
The choristers to control;
The lanners and the merlions
Shall stand in their mourning-gowns;
The hobby and the musket
The censers and the cross shall fet;
The kestrel in all this wark
Shall be holy water clerk.

John Skelton

The Naturalist's Summer-evening Walk

. . . equidem credo, quia sit divinitus illis Ingenium.

VIRGIL *Georgics*

When day declining sheds a milder gleam,
What time the may-fly* haunts the pool or stream;
When the still owl skims round the grassy mead,
What time the timorous hare limps forth to feed;
Then be the time to steal adown the vale,

---

* The angler's may-fly, the *ephemera vulgata Linn.*, comes forth from its aurelia state, and emerges out of the water about six in the evening, and dies about eleven at night, determining the date of its fly state in about five or six hours. They usually begin to appear about the 4th of June, and continue in succession for bear a fortnight. See Swammerdam, Derham, Scopoli, etc.

And listen to the vagrant★ cuckoo's tale;
To hear the clamorous† curlew call his mate,
Or the soft quail his tender pain relate;
To see the swallow sweep the dark'ning plain
Belated, to support her infant train;
To mark the swift in rapid giddy ring
Dash round the steeple, unsubdu'd of wing:
Amusive birds! – say where your hid retreat
When the frost rages and the tempests beat;
Whence your return, by such nice instinct led,
When spring, soft season, lifts her bloomy head?
Such baffled searches mock man's prying pride,
The GOD of NATURE is your secret guide!
  While deep'ning shades obscure the face of day
To yonder bench, leaf-shelter'd, let us stray,
Till blended objects fail the swimming sight,
And all the fading landscape sinks in night;
To hear the drowsy dor come brushing by
With buzzing wing, or the shrill‡ cricket cry;
To see the feeding bat glance through the wood;
To catch the distant falling of the flood;
While o'er the cliff th' awakened churn-owl hung
Through the still gloom protracts his chattering song;
While high in air, and pois'd upon his wings,
Unseen, the soft enamour'd woodlark¶ sings:
These, NATURE's works, the curious mind employ,
Inspire a soothing melancholy joy:
As fancy warms, a pleasing kind of pain
Steals o'er the cheek, and thrills the creeping vein!

★ Vagrant cuckoo; so called because, being tied down by no incubation or
attendance about the nutrition of its young, it wanders without control.
† *Charadrius ædicnemus.*
‡ *Gryllus campestris.*
¶ In hot summer nights woodlarks soar to a prodigious height, and hang
singing in the air.

Each rural sight, each sound, each smell combine;
The tinkling sheep-bell, or the breath of kine;
The new-mown hay that scents the swelling breeze,
Or cottage-chimney smoking through the trees.
  The chilling night-dews fall: away, retire;
For see, the glow-worm lights her amorous fire!*
Thus, ere night's veil had half obscured the sky,
Th' impatient damsel hung her lamp on high:
True to the signal, by love's meteor led,
Leander hasten'd to his Hero's bed.†

I am, etc.
Gilbert White

Under the Hanger
from Gilbert White's Journals

Wood lark whistles. Hogs carry straw.
Sky lark sings.
Young cucumber swells.
Frogs croak: spawn abounds.
Cold & black. Harsh, hazy day.
Backward apples begin to blow.
Frost, sun, fog, rain, snow. Bunting twitters.
No dew, rain, rain, rain.
Swans flounce & dive.
Chilly & dark.
Dark & spitting. Indian flowers in Dec'r!
Ground very wet. The nightingale sings.

---

* The light of the female glow-worm (as she often crawls up the stalk of a grass to make herself more conspicuous) is a signal to the male, which is a slender dusky *scarabœus*.
† See the story of Hero and Leander.

Blackcap sings. The sedge-bird a delicate polyglott.
The titlark begins to sing: a sweet songster!
Turtle coos.
Asparagus begins to sprout.
Cuckoo cries.
No house-martins appear.

Apricots, peaches, & nectarines swell:
sprinkled trees with water, & watered the roots.
Oaks are felled: the bark runs freely.
The leaves of the mulberry trees hardly begin to peep.
Showers, sun & clouds, brisky air.
Much hay spoiled: much not cut.

Put meadow hay in large cock.
Hay well made at last.
Sun, sweet day.

All things in a drowning condition!

First day of winter. Snow on the ground.
Gathered in all the grapes. Snow on the hills.
Full moon.
Rooks resort to their nest-trees.
Grey & sharp.
Earth-worms lie out & copulate.
Great rain. Hops sadly washed.
Ice bears: boys slide.

Rain, rain, rain.

The road in a most dusty, smothering condition.
Full moon. My well is shallow & the water foul.
The grass burns.
A plant of missle-toe grows on a bough of the medlar.
The air is full of insects.

Turkies strut and gobble.
Snow wastes: eaves drip. Cocks crow.
Sun, bright & pleasant.
The boys are playing in their shirts.
Bees thrive. Asparagus abounds.
Dark & chilly, rain. Cold & comfortless.
Mossed the white cucumber bed.
Snow covers the ground.

Planted 12 goose-berry trees, & three monthly roses, &
    three Provence roses.
The voice of the cockow is heard in the hanger.
Grass lamb.
Grey, sprinkling, gleams with thunder.
Wavy, curdled clouds, like the remains of thunder.

Pease are hacked: rye is reaping: turnips thrive & are hoing.
Stifling dust.
Sweet moonshine.
Boys slide on the ice!

Dew, bright, showers: thunder, gleam of sun.
Straw-berries, scarlet, cryed about.
Straw-berries dry, & tasteless.
Taw & hop-scotch come in fashion among the boys.
The sun mounts and looks down on the hanger.
Crown Imperials blow, & stink.
Much gossamer.
Moles work, & heave up their hillocks.
Ice within doors.
Rime.
Snow on the ground.
Snow in the night: snow five inches deep.
Snow on the ground.
Icicles hang in eaves all day.
Snow lies on the hill.

Crocus's make a gaudy show.
Cuculus cuculat: the voice of the cuckoo is heard in
    Blackmoor woods.
The air is filled with floating willow-down.
Fog, sun, pleasant showers, moonshine.
Here & there a wasp.
Black-birds feed on the elder-berries.
Frost, ice, sun pleasant moon-light.
Frost, ice, bright, red even, prodigious white dew.
Thunder, lightening, rain, snow!

Vast damage in various parts!
No frost.
Daffodil blows.

Daffodil blows.
Sweet weather. Mackerel.
Soft wind. The woodpecker laughs.
Cinnamon-roses blow.
Flowers smell well this evening: some dew.
The distant hills look very blue.

Clouds, hail, shower, gleams.
Sharp air, & fire in the parlor.
Sweet day, golden even, red horizon.
Snow-drops, & crocus's shoot.
Vast frost-work on the windows.
Longest day: a cold, harsh solstice!
Thunder & hail.
Yellow evening.
Potatoes blossom.
Men cut their meadows.
Goose-berries wither on the trees.
The seeds of the lime begin to fall.
Grey, & mild, gleams.
Grey, sun, pleasant, yellow even.

Dark & wet.
Rain, rain, gleams. Venus resplendent.
Showers of hail, sleet. Gleams.
The *Cuckoo* is heard on Greatham common.

Cut the first cucumber.
Pulled the first radish.
Early orange-lilies blow.
Cut *five* cucumbers.
Bright, sun, golden even.
Cut *eight* cucumbers.
Provence roses blow against a wall.
Cut *ten* cucumbers.
Dames violets very fine.

Men wash their sheep.

James Schuyler

Blue Booby

The Blue Booby

The blue booby lives
on the bare rocks
of Galápagos
and fears nothing.
It is a simple life:
they live on fish,
and there are few predators.
Also, the males do not
make fools of themselves
chasing after the young
ladies. Rather,
they gather the blue
objects of the world
and construct from them

a nest — an occasional
Gaulois package,
a string of beads,
a piece of cloth from
a sailor's suit. This
replaces the need for
dazzling plumage;
in fact, in the past
fifty million years
the male has grown

considerably duller,
nor can he sing well.
The female, though,

asks little of him —
the blue satisfies her
completely, has
a magical effect
on her. When she returns
from her day of
gossip and shopping,
she sees he has found her
a new shred of blue foil:
for this she rewards him
with her dark body,
the stars turn slowly
in the blue foil beside them
like the eyes of a mild savior.

James Tate

Cormorant

The Common Cormorant

The common cormorant (or shag)
Lays eggs inside a paper bag,
You follow the idea, no doubt?
It's to keep the lightning out.

But what these unobservant birds
Have never thought of, is that herds
Of wandering bears might come with buns
And steal the bags to hold the crumbs.

Christopher Isherwood

To be Engraved on the Skull of a Cormorant

across the thin
façade, the galleried-
with-membrane head:
narrowing, to take
the eye-dividing
declivity where
the beginning beak
prepares for flight
in a still-
perfect salience:

here, your glass
needs must stay
steady and your gross
needle re-tip
itself with reticence
but be
as searching as the sea
that picked and pared
this head yet spared
its frail acuity.

Charles Tomlinson

Grey Heron

The Heron

One of the most begrudging avian take-offs
is the heron's *fucking hell, all right, all right,*
I'll go to the garage for your flaming fags
cranky departure, though once they're up
their flight can be extravagant. I watched
one big spender climb the thermal staircase,
a calorific waterspout of frogs
and sticklebacks, the undercarriage down
and trailing. Seen from antiquity
you gain the Icarus thing; seen from my childhood
that cursing man sets out for Superkings,
though the heron cares for neither as it struggles
into its wings then soars sunwards and throws
its huge overcoat across the earth.

Paul Farley

Heron

It's evening on the river,
steady, milk-warm,

the nettles head-down
with feasting caterpillars,

the current turning,
thin as a blade-bone.

Reed-mace shivers.
I'm miles from anywhere.

Who's looking?
did a fish jump?

– and then a heron goes up
from its place by the willow.

With ballooning flight
it picks up the sky

and makes off, loaded.
I wasn't looking,

I heard the noise of its wings
and I turned,

I thought of a friend,
a cool one with binoculars,

here's rarity
with big wing-flaps, suiting itself.

Helen Dunmore

Mute Swan

Leda and the Swan

A sudden blow: the great wings beating still
Above the staggering girl, her thighs caressed
By the dark webs, her nape caught in his bill,
He holds her helpless breast upon his breast.

How can those terrified vague fingers push
The feathered glory from her loosening thighs?
And how can body, laid in that white rush,
But feel the strange heart beating where it lies?

A shudder in the loins engenders there
The broken wall, the burning roof and tower
And Agamemnon dead.
               Being so caught up,
So mastered by the brute blood of the air,
Did she put on his knowledge with his power
Before the indifferent beak could let her drop?

                        W. B. Yeats

Whooper Swan

The Wild Swans at Coole

The trees are in their autumn beauty,
The woodland paths are dry,
Under the October twilight the water
Mirrors a still sky;
Upon the brimming water among the stones
Are nine-and-fifty swans.

The nineteenth autumn has come upon me
Since I first made my count;
I saw, before I had well finished,
All suddenly mount
And scatter wheeling in great broken rings
Upon their clamorous wings.

I have looked upon those brilliant creatures,
And now my heart is sore.
All's changed since I, hearing at twilight,
The first time on this shore,
The bell-beat of their wings above my head,
Trod with a lighter tread.

Unwearied still, lover by lover,
They paddle in the cold
Companionable streams or climb the air;
Their hearts have not grown old;
Passion or conquest, wander where they will,
Attend upon them still.

But now they drift on the still water,
Mysterious, beautiful;
Among what rushes will they build,
By what lake's edge or pool
Delight men's eyes when I awake some day
To find they have flown away?

W. B. Yeats

Postscript

And some time make the time to drive out west
Into County Clare, along the Flaggy Shore,
In September or October, when the wind
And the light are working off each other
So that the ocean on one side is wild
With foam and glitter, and inland among stones
The surface of a slate-grey lake is lit
By the earthed lightning of a flock of swans,
Their feathers roughed and ruffling, white on white,
Their fully grown headstrong-looking heads
Tucked or cresting or busy underwater.
Useless to think you'll park and capture it
More thoroughly. You are neither here nor there,
A hurry through which known and strange things pass
As big soft buffetings come at the car sideways
And catch the heart off guard and blow it open.

Seamus Heaney

Goose

The Old Grey Goose

Go and tell Aunt Nancy,
Go and tell Aunt Nancy,
Go and tell Aunt Nancy
The old grey goose is dead.

The one that she'd been saving
For to make her feather-bed.

She died last Friday
With a pain all in her head.

Old gander is weeping
Because his wife is dead.

The goslings are mourning
Because their mother's dead.

Anonymous

Skeins o Geese

Skeins o geese write a word
across the sky. A word
struck lik a gong
afore I wis born.
The sky moves like cattle, lowin.

I'm as empty as stane, as fields
ploo'd but not sown, naked
an blin as a stane. Blin
tae the word, blin
tae a' soon but geese ca'ing.

Wire twists lik archaic script
roon a gate. The barbs
sign tae the wind as though
it was deef. The word whustles
ower high for ma senses. Awa.

No lik the past which lies
strewn aroun. Nor sudden death.
No like a lover we'll ken
an connect wi forever.
The hem of its goin drags across the sky.

Whit dae birds write on the dusk?
A word niver spoken or read.
The skeins turn hame,
on the wind's dumb moan, a soun,
maybe human, bereft.

Kathleen Jamie

Wigeon

Widgeon

(for Paul Muldoon)

It had been badly shot.
While he was plucking it
he found, he says, the voice box —

like a flute stop
in the broken windpipe —

and blew upon it
unexpectedly
his own small widgeon cries.

Seamus Heaney

Mandarin Duck

Mandarin Duck

The box of a frozen-food tiramisu misfolded into a crumple.
Looking for its reading glasses. Feral in Surrey.

Richard Price

Deaths & Depletions 1

The Death and Burial of Cock Robbin

'And who catch'd his blood?'
'I' said the fish, 'with my little dish,
And I catch'd his blood.'

'And who did make his shroud?'
'I' said the beetle, 'with my little needle,
And I did make his shroud.'

'Who'll dig his grave?'
'I' said the owl,
'With my spade and show'l,
And I'll dig his grave.'

'Who'll be the parson?'
'I' said the rook,
'With my little book,
And I'll be the parson.'

'Who'll be the clerk?'
'I' said the lark,
'If 'tis not in the dark,
And I'll be the clerk.'

'Who'll carry him to the grave?'
'I' said the kite,
'If 'tis not in the night,
And I'll carry him to the grave.'

'Who'll carry the link?'
'I' said the linnet,
'I'll fetch it in a minute,
And I'll carry the link.'

'Who'll be chief mourner?'
'I' said the swan,
'I'm sorry he's gone,
And I'll be chief mourner.'

'Who'll bear the pall?'
'We' said the wren,
Both the cock and the hen,
'And we'll bear the pall.'

'Who'll run before?'
'I' said the deer,
'I run fast for fear,
And I'll run before.'

'Who'll sing a psalm?'
'I' said the thrush,
As she sat in a bush,
'And I'll sing a psalm.'

'Who'll throw in the dirt?'
'I' said the fox,
'Though I steal hens and cocks,
I'll throw in the dirt.'

'And who'll toll the bell?'
'I' said the bull,
'Because I can pull,
And so, Cock Robbin, farewell!'

All the birds of the air
Fell to sighing and sobbing,
When they heard the bell toll
For poor Cock Robbin.

Anonymous

The Archaeopteryx's Song

I am only half out of this rock of scales.
What good is armour when you want to fly?
My tail is like a stony pedestal
and not a rudder. If I sit back on it
I sniff winds, clouds, rains, fogs where
I'd be, where I'd be flying, be flying high.
Dinosaurs are spicks and
all I see when I look back
is tardy turdy bonehead swamps
whose scruples are dumb tons.
Damnable plates and plaques
can't even keep out ticks.
They think when they make the ground thunder
as they lumber for a horn-lock or a rut
that someone is afraid, that everyone is afraid,
but no one is afraid. The lords of creation
are in my mate's next egg's next egg's next egg,
stegosaur. It's feathers I need, more feathers
for the life to come. And these iron teeth
I want away, and a smooth beak

to cut the air. And these claws
on my wings, what use are they
except to drag me down, do you imagine
I am ever going to crawl again?
When I first left that crag
and flapped low and heavy over the ravine
I saw past present and future
like a dying tyrannosaur
and skimmed it with a hiss.
I will teach my sons and daughters to live
on mist and fire and fly to the stars.

Edwin Morgan

That find of *Longisquama insignis*,

oldest known feathered fossil evidence,
from a reptilian creature which most likely
glided between the trees in forest swamps
75 million years pre-*Archaeopterix*
in Central Asia, anticipated birds.

It had a furcula virtually the same
as modern birds, and *wasn't* a dinosaur.

What was the initial function of those feathers
(whose evolution probably antedates
the dinosaur)? Did they develop from scales
for insulation when warm blood arrived?

Or did these nascent plumes burgeon from ridges
along the back, and muscles then develop
in forelimbs, coincident with plumage growth,
enabling first flight? . . .

Sunt aliquid manes.

Peter Reading

The Last Moa

Somewhere in the bush, the last moa
is not still lingering in some hidden valley.
She is not stretching her swanlike neck
(but longer, more massive than any swan's)
for a high cluster of miro berries,
or grubbing up fern roots with her beak.

Alice McKenzie didn't see her
among the sandhills at Martin's Bay
in 1880 – a large blue bird
as tall as herself, which turned and chased her.
Moas were taller than seven-year-old
pioneer children; moas weren't blue.

Twenty or thirty distinct species –
all of them, even the small bush moa,
taller than Alice – and none of their bones
carbon-dated to less than five centuries.
The sad, affronted mummified head
in the museum is as old as a Pharaoh.

Not the last moa, that; but neither
was Alice's harshly grunting pursuer.
Possibly Alice met a takahe:
the extinct bird that rose from extinction
in 1948, near Te Anau.
No late reprieve, though, for the moa.

Her thigh-bones, longer than a giraffe's,
are lying steeped in a swamp, or smashed
in a midden, with her unstrung vertebrae.
Our predecessors hunted and ate her,
gobbled her up: as we'd have done
in their place; as we're gobbling the world.

                                        Fleur Adcock

Passenger Pigeon

The bird's sad demise is chronicled on many websites. Children
Visit these for homework, and learn how far and fast the
    passenger pigeon
Flew, and that its breast was red, and head and rump slate blue.

As the opulent sun set, raccoon-hatted hunters would gather
    with pots
Of sulphur, and clubs and poles and ladders; in a trice they'd
    transform the dung-
Heaped forest floor into a two-foot carpet of smouldering
    pigeon.

                                        Mark Ford

Eagle

The Dalliance of the Eagles

Skirting the river road, (my forenoon walk, my rest,)
Skyward in air a sudden muffled sound, the dalliance of the
    eagles,
The rushing amorous contact high in space together,
The clinching interlocking claws, a living, fierce, gyrating wheel,
Four beating wings, two beaks, a swirling mass tight grappling,
In tumbling turning clustering loops, straight downward falling,
Till o'er the river pois'd, the twain yet one, a moment's lull,
A motionless still balance in the air, then parting, talons loosing,
Upward again on slow-firm pinions slanting, their separate
    diverse flight,
She hers, he his, pursuing.

Walt Whitman

Red Kite

Red Kites at Tregaron

They know where to find me when they want to feed.
At dusk I prepare, lay out the fat

and spread unspeakable offal in snow
like scarlet necklaces. They know

how to find me. They are my words
for beauty and other birds

fight them, vulgar, down threads of air
which bring them to me. They brawl for hair,

for skin, torn giblets and gizzard which I
provide for them, domestic. Inside

the house is so cold I can see my breath,
my face in the polished oak. My mouth

is sweet with silence. Talon and claw
are tender to me, the craw

much kinder than men. What is most foul
in me kites love. At night I feel

their clear minds stirring in rowan and oak
out in the desert. I stroke

the counterpane, my sleepless skies
filled with the stars of untameable eyes.

Gwyneth Lewis

Secretary Bird

Secretary Bird

Its name describes it, even to those penholder patches
Behind pale ears, the desiccated manner, head tilted
Back, offended, supercilious as it scratches
The scrub for snakes, faltering on stork-stilted
Legs feathered grey-black with tatty patches.

No other name could so well have drawn
Forth the image, as I saw it, near Philippolis, alone
Among thornbushes, in the red earth sharp stones
And waterwheels glinting, but in the whole Karoo
Only it moving, though abstracted, wondering what to do.

Since Kroonstad, 500 miles back, nothing so human
Had stirred in the desert, no man nor carrying woman,
So that stopping my car I had jumped it nearer
Through glasses, as on inadequate legs it came clearer,
Uncertainly swerving, as if blown by the dust.

And something about that haphazard swerve must
Have caught my memory, jolting me suddenly back
To a sailboat of a girl, quite incongruously unlike
It, but who moved so – indelibly so –,
Through a part of my life, a long time ago.
I smiled at the absurdity, to find, as I let
In the clutch, my cheeks unaccountably wet.

Alan Ross

Hawk

The Hawk

On Sunday the hawk fell on Bigging
    And a chicken screamed
    Lost in its own little snowstorm.
And on Monday he fell on the moor
    And the Field Club
    Raised a hundred silent prisms.
And on Tuesday he fell on the hill
    And the happy lamb
    Never knew why the loud collie straddled him.
And on Wednesday he fell on a bush
    And the blackbird
    Laid by his little flute for the last time.
And on Thursday he fell on Cleat
    And peerie Tom's rabbit
    Swung in a single arc from shore to hill.
And on Friday he fell on a ditch
    But the rampant rat,
    That eye and that tooth, quenched his flame.
And on Saturday he fell on Bigging
    And Jock lowered his gun
    And nailed a small wing over the corn.

George Mackay Brown

Falcon

Hawk Roosting

I sit in the top of the wood, my eyes closed.
Inaction, no falsifying dream
Between my hooked head and hooked feet:
Or in sleep rehearse perfect kills and eat.

The convenience of the high trees!
The air's buoyancy and the sun's ray
Are of advantage to me;
And the earth's face upward for my inspection.

My feet are locked upon the rough bark.
It took the whole of Creation
To produce my foot, my each feather:
Now I hold Creation in my foot

Or fly up, and revolve it all slowly –
I kill where I please because it is all mine.
There is no sophistry in my body:
My manners are tearing off heads –

The allotment of death.
For the one path of my flight is direct
Through the bones of the living.
No arguments assert my right:

The sun is behind me.
Nothing has changed since I began.
My eye has permitted no change.
I am going to keep things like this.

Ted Hughes

Tamer and Hawk

I thought I was so tough,
But gentled at your hands
Cannot be quick enough
To fly for you and show
That when I go I go
At your commands.

Even in flight above
I am no longer free:
You seeled me with your love,
I am blind to other birds –
The habit of your words
Has hooded me.

As formerly, I wheel
I hover and I twist,
But only want the feel
In my possessive thought,
Of catcher and of caught
Upon your wrist.

You but half–civilize,
Taming me in this way.
Through having only eyes
For you I fear to lose,
I lose to keep, and choose
Tamer as prey.

Thom Gunn

Kestrel

The Windhover
To Christ our Lord

I caught this morning morning's minion, king-
   dom of daylight's dauphin, dapple-dawn-drawn Falcon, in his
     riding
   Of the rolling level underneath him steady air, and striding
High there, how he rung upon the rein of a wimpling wing
In his ecstasy! then off, off forth on swing,
   As a skate's heel sweeps smooth on a bow-bend: the hurl and
     gliding
   Rebuffed the big wind. My heart in hiding
Stirred for a bird, – the achieve of, the mastery of the thing!

Brute beauty and valour and act, oh, air, pride, plume, here
   Buckle! AND the fire that breaks from thee then, a billion
Times told lovelier, more dangerous, O my chevalier!

   No wonder of it: shéer plód makes plough down sillion
Shine, and blue-bleak embers, ah my dear,
   Fall, gall themselves, and gash gold-vermilion.

Gerard Manley Hopkins

A Day Out 2

Song

What Bird so sings, yet so dos wayle?
O t'is the rauish'd Nightingale.
Iug, Iug, Iug, Iug, tereu, shee cryes,
And still her woes at Midnight rise.
Braue prick song! who is't now we heare?
None but the Larke so shrill and cleare;
How at heauens gats she claps her wings,
The Morne no waking till shee sings.
Heark, heark, with what a pretty throat
Poore Robin red-breast tunes his note;
Hear how the iolly Cuckoes sing
Cuckoe, to welcome in the spring,
Cuckoe, to welcome in the spring.

John Lyly

Birds in Alarm

The fire tail tells the boys when nests are nigh
And tweets and flyes from every passer bye
The yellow hammer never makes a noise
But flyes in silence from the noisey boys
The boys will come and take them every day
And still she lays as none were taen away

The nightingale keeps tweeting churring round
But leaves in silence when the nest is found
The pewet hollos chewsit as she flyes
And flops about the shepherd where he lies
But when her nest is found she stops her song
And cocks [her] coppled crown and runs along
Wrens cock their tails and chitter loud and play
And robins hollow tut and flye away

John Clare

'There was an Old Man with a beard'

There was an Old Man with a beard,
Who said, 'It is just as I feared! –
Two Owls and a Hen, four Larks and a Wren,
Have all built their nests in my beard.'

Edward Lear

Birds

There were small birds would fly in the trenches at times,
Loved to our Gloucester eyes –
Who would see with surprise
Some visitor from home with a touch of rhymes
Ending a talk and poetry becoming easy and wise.
These were the hedge sparrows / (music) / by Maisemore, Her
    green
Small hill, and Minsterworth starlings flocking in clouds
Of whirring black ones on the gold stubble and half seen
Lovely weeds of hearts ease, pimpernel, ladies bedstraw.

Blackbirds of Wellington Street; matthw of Leadon's law,
One kingfisher, one laughing linnet in the shrouds
Of April, under the luminous azure white heaven's measure.
Linnets with wavering flight going over Corse way to delight
Boy with as sure
A sense of earth as any of ~~the~~ birds – but earths friend and
more
So some good Spirit friended to the music or verse ended.
There was a yellow hammer by Hartpury manor
And robins by High Hartbury were good as crumbs to me.
(Had I been robin – or yellow hammer a loving human.)
(If crumbs are dear to robins like the heart's touch of humans)
~~Or~~ they were my brothers, but I a prince above others,
Having music within my blood, verse eager to say my mood.
The fire of sword and steel shine with pity of a woman.

Ivor Gurney

Over Sir John's Hill

Over Sir John's hill,
The hawk on fire hangs still;
In a hoisted cloud, at drop of dusk, he pulls to his claws
And gallows, up the rays of his eyes the small birds of the bay
And the shrill child's play
Wars
Of the sparrows and such who swansing, dusk, in wrangling
hedges.
And blithely they squawk
To fiery tyburn over the wrestle of elms until
The flash the noosed hawk
Crashes, and slowly the fishing holy stalking heron
In the river Towy below bows his tilted headstone.

Flash, and the plumes crack,
And a black cap of jack-
Daws Sir John's just hill dons, and again the gulled birds hare
To the hawk on fire, the halter height, over Towy's fins,
In a whack of wind.
There
Where the elegiac fisherbird stabs and paddles
In the pebbly dab-filled
Shallow and sedge, and 'dilly dilly,' calls the loft hawk,
'Come and be killed,'
I open the leaves of the water at a passage
Of psalms and shadows among the pincered sandcrabs prancing

And read, in a shell,
Death clear as a buoy's bell:
All praise of the hawk on fire in hawk-eyed dusk be sung,
When his viperish fuse hangs looped with flames under the brand
Wing, and blest shall
Young
Green chickens of the bay and bushes cluck, 'dilly dilly,
Come let us die.'
We grieve as the blithe birds, never again, leave shingle and elm,
The heron and I,
I young Aesop fabling to the near night by the dingle
Of eels, saint heron hymning in the shell-hung distant

Crystal harbour vale
Where the sea cobbles sail,
And wharves of water where the walls dance and the white
    cranes stilt.
It is the heron and I, under judging Sir John's elmed
Hill, tell-tale the knelled
Guilt
Of the led-astray birds whom God, for their breast of whistles,
Have mercy on,
God in his whirlwind silence save, who marks the sparrows hail,

For their souls' song.
Now the heron grieves in the weeded verge. Through windows
Of dusk and water I see the tilting whispering
Heron, mirrored, go,
As the snapt feathers snow,
Fishing in the tear of the Towy. Only a hoot owl
Hollows, a grassblade blown in cupped hands, in the looted elms
And no green cocks or hens
Shout
Now on Sir John's hill. The heron, ankling the scaly
Lowlands of the waves,
Makes all the music; and I who hear the tune of the slow,
Wear-willow river, grave,
Before the lunge of the night, the notes on this time-shaken
Stone for the sake of the souls of the slain birds sailing.

Dylan Thomas

Birdsong for Two Voices

A spiral ascending the morning,
climbing by means of a song into the sun,
to be sung reciprocally by two birds at intervals
in the same tree but not quite in time.

A song that assembles the earth
out of nine notes and silence.
out of the unformed gloom before dawn
where every tree is a problem to be solved by birdsong.

Crex Crex Corcorovado,
letting the pieces fall where they may,
every dawn divides into the distinct
misgiving between alternate voices

sung repeatedly by two birds at intervals
out of nine notes and silence,
while the sun, with its fingers to the earth,
as the sun proceeds so it gathers instruments:

it gathers the yard with its echoes and scaffolding sounds,
it gathers the swerving away sound of the road,
it gathers the river shivering in a wet field,
it gathers the three small bones in the dark of the eardrum;

it gathers the big bass silence of clouds
and the mind whispering in its shell
and all trees, with their ears to the air,
seeking a steady state and singing it over till it settles.

Alice Oswald

Turkey

Turkey-Cock

You ruffled black blossom,
You glossy dark wind.

Your sort of gorgeousness,
Dark and lustrous
And skinny repulsive
And poppy-glossy,
Is the gorgeousness that evokes my most puzzled admiration.

Your aboriginality
Deep, unexplained,
Like a Red Indian darkly unfinished and aloof,
Seems like the black and glossy seeds of countless centuries.

Your wattles are the colour of steel-slag which has been
    red-hot
And is going cold,
Cooling to a powdery, pale-oxidised sky-blue.

Why do you have wattles, and a naked, wattled head?
Why do you arch your naked-set eye with a more-
    than-comprehensible arrogance?

The vulture is bald, so is the condor, obscenely,
But only you have thrown this amazing mantilla of oxidised
    sky-blue
And hot red over you.

This queer dross shawl of blue and vermilion,
Whereas the peacock has a diadem.

I wonder why.
Perhaps it is a sort of uncanny decoration, a veil of loose skin.
Perhaps it is your assertion, in all this ostentation, of raw
    contradictoriness.
Your wattles drip down like a shawl to your breast
And the point of your mantilla drops across your nose,
    unpleasantly.

Or perhaps it is something unfinished
A bit of slag still adhering, after your firing in the furnace of
    creation.

Or perhaps there is something in your wattles of a bull's
    dew-lap
Which slips down like a pendulum to balance the throbbing mass
    of a generous breast,
The over-drip of a great passion hanging in the balance.
Only yours would be a raw, unsmelted passion, that will not
    quite fuse from the dross.

You contract yourself,
You arch yourself as an archer's bow
Which quivers indrawn as you clench your spine
Until your veiled head almost touches backward
To the root-rising of your erected tail.
And one intense and backward-curving frisson
Seizes you as you clench yourself together
Like some fierce magnet bringing its poles together.

Burning, pale positive pole of your wattled head!
And from the darkness of that opposite one
The upstart of your round-barred, sun-round tail!

Whilst between the two, along the tense arch of your back
Blows the magnetic current in fierce blasts,
Ruffling black, shining feathers like lifted mail,
Shuddering storm wind, or a water rushing through.

Your brittle, super-sensual arrogance
Tosses the crape of red across your brow and down your
    breast
As you draw yourself upon yourself in insistence.

It is a declaration of such tension in will
As time has not dared to avouch, nor eternity been able to
    unbend
Do what it may.
A raw American will, that has never been tempered by life;
You brittle, will-tense bird with a foolish eye.

The peacock lifts his rods of bronze
And struts blue-brilliant out of the far East.
But watch a turkey prancing low on earth
Drumming his vaulted wings, as savages drum
Their rhythms on long-drawn, hollow, sinister drums.
The ponderous, sombre sound of the great drum of Huichilobos
In pyramid Mexico, during sacrifice.
Drum, and the turkey onrush,
Sudden, demonic dauntlessness, full abreast,
All the bronze gloss of all his myriad petals
Each one apart and instant.
Delicate frail crescent of the gentle outline of white
At each feather-tip
So delicate;
Yet the bronze wind-bell suddenly clashing
And the eye over-weening into madness.

Turkey-cock, turkey-cock
Are you the bird of the next dawn?

Has the peacock had his day, does he call in vain, screecher,
      for the sun to rise?
The eagle, the dove, and the barnyard rooster, do they call in
      vain, trying to wake the morrow?
And do you await us, wattled father, Westward?
Will your yell do it?

Take up the trail of the vanished American
Where it disappeared at the foot of the crucifix?
Take up the primordial Indian obstinacy,
The more than human, dense insistence of will,
And disdain, and blankness, and onrush, and prise open the new
      day with them?

The East a dead letter, and Europe moribund . . . Is that so?
And those sombre, dead, feather-lustrous Aztecs,
      Amerindians,
In all the sinister splendour of their red blood-sacrifices,
Do they stand under the dawn, half-godly, half-demon, awaiting
      the cry of the turkey-cock?

Or must you go through the fire once more, till you're smelted
      pure,
Slag-wattled turkey-cock,
Dross-jabot?

                                                    D. H. Lawrence

Cock and Hen

On a Cock at Rochester

Thou cursed Cock, with thy perpetual Noise,
May'st thou be Capon made, and lose thy Voice,
Or on a Dunghil may'st thou spend thy Blood,
And Vermin prey upon thy craven Brood;
May Rivals tread thy Hens before thy Face,
Then with redoubled Courage give thee chase;
May'st thou be punish'd for *St. Peter*'s Crime,
And on *Shrove-tuesday*, perish in thy Prime;
May thy bruis'd Carcass be some Beggar's Feast,
Thou first and worst Disturber of Man's Rest.

Sir Charles Sedley

Cock-Crow

Out of the wood of thoughts that grows by night
To be cut down by the sharp axe of light, –
Out of the night, two cocks together crow,
Cleaving the darkness with a silver blow:
And bright before my eyes twin trumpeters stand,
Heralds of splendour, one at either hand,
Each facing each as in a coat of arms:
The milkers lace their boots up at the farms.

Edward Thomas

To a Prize Bird

You suit me well; for you can make me laugh,
Nor are you blinded by the chaff
    That every wind sends spinning from the rick.

You know to think, and what you think you speak
With much of Samson's pride and bleak
    Finality; and none dare bid you stop.

Pride sits you well, so strut, colossal bird.
No barnyard makes you look absurd;
    Your brazen claws are staunch against defeat.

Marianne Moore

Cock-Crows

I stood on a dark summit, among dark summits –
Tidal dawn splitting heaven from earth,
The oyster
Opening to taste gold.

And I heard the cock-crows kindling in the valley
Under the mist –
They were sleepy,
Bubbling deep in the valley cauldron.

Then one or two tossed clear, like soft rockets
And sank back again dimming.

Then soaring harder, brighter, higher
Tearing the mist,
Bubble-glistenings flung up and bursting to light
Brightening the undercloud,
The fire crests of the cocks – the sickle shouts,
Challenge against challenge, answer to answer,
Hooking higher,
Clambering up the sky as they melted,
Hanging smouldering from the night's fringes.

Till the whole valley brimmed with cock-crows,
A magical soft mixture boiling over,
Spilling and sparkling into other valleys

Lobbed-up horse-shoes of glow-swollen metal
From sheds in back-gardens, hen-cotes, farms
Sinking back mistily

Till the last spark died, and embers paled

And the sun climbed into its wet sack
For the day's work

While the dark rims hardened
Over the smoke of towns, from holes in earth.

Ted Hughes

The Chicken without a Head

1

When two times two was three,
The chicken without a head was hatched.
When the earth was still flat,
It fell off its edge, daydreaming.
When there were 13 signs in the zodiac,
It found a dead star for its gizzard.
When the first fox was getting married,
It taught itself to fly with one wing.
When all the eggs were still golden,
The clouds in the sky tasted like sweet corn.
When the rain flooded its coop,
Its wishbone was its ark.
Ah, when the chicken had only itself to roast,
The lightning was its skewer,
The thunder its baste and salt.

2

The chicken without a head made a sigh,
And then a hailstone out of that sigh,
And the window for the hailstone to strike.
Nine lives it made for itself,
And nine coats of solitude to dress them in.
It made its own shadow. No, I'm lying.
It only made a flea to bite some holes in the shadow.
Made it all out of nothing. Made a needle
To sew back its broken eggshell.
Made the lovers naked. Everybody else put clothes on them.
Its father made the knife, but it polished the blade,
Until it threw back its image like a funhouse mirror.
Made it all out of raglets of time.
Who's to say it'd be happier if it didn't?

3

Hear the song of a chicken without a head
As it goes scratching in grave dirt.
A song in which two parallel lines
Meet at infinity, in which God
Makes the last of the little apples,
In which golden fleece is heard growing
On a sad girl's pubes. The song
of swearwords dreaming of a pure mouth.
The song of a doornail raised from the dead.
The song of circumspection because accomplices
Have been found, because the egg's safe
In the cuckoo's nest. The song
You wade into until your own hat floats.
A song of contagious laughter.
A lethal song.
That's right, the song of premonition.

4

On a headless evening of a headless day
The chicken on fire and the words
Around it like a ring of fabulous beasts.
Each night it threw them a bite-size portion of its heart.
The words were hungry, the night held the fork.
Whatever our stylish gallows bird made, its head unmade,
Its long-lost, axed-off sultan's head
Rose into the sky in a balloon of fiery numerals.
Down below the great feast went on:
The table that supplies itself with bread.
A saw that cuts a dream in half.
Wings so quick they don't get wet in heavy rain.
The egg that mutters to the frying pan:
I swear it by the hair in my yolk,
There's no such thing as a chicken without a head.

5

The chicken without a head ran a maze,
Ran half-plucked,
A serving fork stuck in its back,
Ran, backward, into the blue of the evening.
Ran upside down,
Its drumsticks and talons in the clouds.
Someone huge and red-aproned rose in its wake.
Many black umbrellas parting to let it pass.
Ran leaving its squinting head far behind,
Its head reeking of barber's cologne.
Ran up the church steeple,
Up the lightning rod on that steeple
For the wind to hone its prettiest plumes.
Ran, and is still running this Good Friday,
Between raindrops,
Hellfoxes on its trail.

Charles Simic

Capercaillie

Capercaillies

In a deep, in a dark wood, somewhere north of Loch Lomond,
Saint Joan and I should be in our element;
the electroplated bracken and furze
have only gradually given way to pines and firs

in which a – what? – a straggler from Hadrian's
sixth legion squats over the latrine
and casts a die. His spurs suggest a renegade
Norman knight, as does his newly-prinked

escutcheon of sable on a field of sable,
whereas the hens – three, four, five – in fashionable
yellow gum-boots, are meekly back from Harrods.
Once a year (tonight, perhaps) such virtue has its reward;

raising his eyes to heaven – as if about to commit hara-
kiri – the cock will hop on each in turn and, unhurri-
edly, do three or four push-ups,
reaching all too soon for a scuffed Elizabeth Bishop.

'Paul? Was it you put the *pol* in polygamy
or was it somebody else?' While their flesh is notably gamey
even in bilberry-time, their winter tack's
mainly pine-shoots, so they now smack

of nothing so much as turpentine.
Room 233. Through a frosted, half-opened
window I listen to the love-burps and borborygms of a
    capercaillie
('horse of the woods', the name means in Gaelic)

as he challenges me to mortal combat.
The following morning, Saint Joan has moved into the
    camp-bed.

Paul Muldoon

Pheasant

Pheasant

You said you would kill it this morning.
Do not kill it. It startles me still,
The jut of that odd, dark head, pacing

Through the uncut grass on the elm's hill.
It is something to own a pheasant,
Or just to be visited at all.

I am not mystical: it isn't
As if I thought it had a spirit.
It is simply in its element.

That gives it a kingliness, a right.
The print of its big foot last winter,
The tail-track, on the snow in our court –

The wonder of it, in that pallor,
Through crosshatch of sparrow and starling.
Is it its rareness, then? It is rare.

But a dozen would be worth having,
A hundred, on that hill – green and red,
Crossing and recrossing: a fine thing!

It is such a good shape, so vivid.
It's a little cornucopia.
It unclaps, brown as a leaf, and loud,

Settles in the elm, and is easy.
It was sunning in the narcissi.
I trespass stupidly. Let be, let be.

                                        Sylvia Plath

Corncrake

The Corn Craiks Rispy Song

The corncraik rispt her summer call Just as the sun went down
Copper red a burning ball In woods behind the town
I wandered forth a maid to meet So bonny and so fair
No other flower was half so sweet And cole black was her hair

Upon the grasses stood the dew Bead drop O' clearest pearl
Her hair was black her eyes were blue O what a lovely Girl
Her neck was like the lilly white Her breast was like the swan
She was in heart and loves delight A worship for a Man

The corncraiks rispy song was oer The sun had left the light
[alone]
I love dusk kisses on the Moor To lewder life unknown
Hid in the bosom of a flower Its lifetime there to dwell
Eternity would seem an hour And I'd be resting well

John Clare

The Landrail

How sweet and pleasant grows the way
Through summer time again
While Landrails call from day to day
Amid the grass and grain

We hear it in the weeding time
When knee deep waves the corn
We hear it in the summers prime
Through meadows night and morn

And now I hear it in the grass
That grows as sweet again
And let a minutes notice pass
And now tis in the grain

Tis like a fancy every where
A sort of living doubt
We know tis something but it neer
Will blab the secret out

If heard in close or meadow plots
It flies if we pursue
But follows if we notice not
The close and meadow through

Boys know the note of many a bird
In their birdnesting bounds
But when the landrails noise is heard
They wonder at the sounds

They look in every tuft of grass
Thats in their rambles met
They peep in every bush they pass
And none the wiser yet

And still they hear the craiking sound
And still they wonder why
It surely cant be under ground
Nor is it in the sky

And yet tis heard in every vale
An undiscovered song
And makes a pleasant wonder tale
For all the summer long

The shepherd whistles through his hands
And starts with many a whoop
His busy dog across the lands
In hopes to fright it up

Tis still a minutes length or more
Till dogs are off and gone
Then sings and louder than before
But keeps the secret on

Yet accident will often meet
The nest within its way
And weeders when they weed the wheat
Discover where they lay

And mowers on the meadow lea
Chance on their noisy guest
And wonder what the bird can be
That lays without a nest

In simple holes that birds will rake
When dusting in the ground
They drop their eggs of curious make
Deep blotched and nearly round

A mystery still to men and boys
Who knows not where they lay
And guess it but a summer noise
Among the meadow hay

John Clare

First Corncrake

We heard the corncrake's call from close at hand,
and took the lane that led us near the noise;
a hedged half-acre, flanked by sycamore,
was his small wedge of world. We crouched and peered
through the close thorn. The moving cry again
swivelled our gaze. Time whispered in the leaves.
A tall ditch-grass blade rocked as a languid bee
brushed the dry sliver with a rasping wing.

In silence still we watched; a careless heel
smashing a twig husk, grating on the grit,
and winning for itself a warning glance.
Then, when strung patience seemed about to yawn
as if the world demanded leave to move
on its slung reeling pitch about the sun,
I saw a head, a narrow pointed head
stirring among the brown weed-mottled grass
as the monotonous and edgy voice
kept up its hard complaint. I held the spot
in a fixed gaze. The brown head disappeared,
was seen in seconds in another clump,
and for a blessed moment, full in sight
the brown bird, brighter than the book foresaw,
stood calling in a little pool of grass.
I moved a finger and you shared the joy
that chance till then had never offered us.

It would have been a little grief to know
this punctual cry each year, and yet grow old
without one glimpse of him that made the cry.
The heart still hankers for the rounded shape.

John Hewitt

Corncrakes

Incorrigible, unmusical,
They bridged the surrounding hedge of my childhood,
Unsubtle, the opposite of blackbirds,
But, unlike blackbirds, capable
Anywhere they are of endorsing summer
Like loud men around the corner
Whom we never see but whose raucous
Voices can give us confidence.

Louis MacNeice

A Voice of Summer

In this one of all fields I know the best
All day and night, hoarse and melodious, sounded
A creeping corncrake, coloured like the ground,
Till the cats got him and gave the rough air rest.

Mechanical August, dowdy in the reeds,
He ground his quern and the round minutes sifted
Away in the powdery light. He would never lift
His beady periscope over the dusty hayseeds.

Cunning low-runner, tobogganing on his breast
He slid from sight once, from my feet. He only
Became the grass; then stone scraped harsh on stone,
Boxing the compass round his trivial nest.

– Summer now is diminished, is less by him.
Something that it could say cannot be spoken –
As though the language of a subtle folk
Had lost a word that had no synonym.

Norman MacCaig

Deaths & Depletions 2

Bird Scaring Rhymes

Hi! Shoo all o' the birds
   Shoo aller birds
   Shoo aller birds

Out of master's ground
Into Tom Tucker's ground

Out of Tom Tucker's ground
Into Tom Tinker's ground

Out of Tom Tinker's ground
Into Luke Collis' ground

Out of Luke Collis' ground
Into Bill Vater's ground

Hi! Shoo aller birds
Kraw! Hoop!

———

Vlee away, blackie cap,
Don't ye hurt measter's crap,
While I vil my tatie-trap
And lie down and teak a nap.

———

Pigeons and crows
Take care of your toes,
Or I'll pick up my crackers,
And knock you down backwards.
Shoo all away, shoo away, shoo.

Anonymous

The Blinded Bird

So zestfully canst thou sing?
And all this indignity,
With God's consent, on thee!
Blinded ere yet a-wing
By the red-hot needle thou,
I stand and wonder how
So zestfully thou canst sing!

Resenting not such wrong,
Thy grievous pain forgot,
Eternal dark thy lot,
Groping thy whole life long,
After that stab of fire;
Enjailed in pitiless wire;
Resenting not such wrong!

Who hath charity? This bird.
Who suffereth long and is kind,
Is not provoked, though blind
And alive ensepulchred?
Who hopeth, endureth all things?
Who thinketh no evil, but sings?
Who is divine? This bird.

Thomas Hardy

Song Composed in August

Now westlin winds, and slaught'ring guns
    Bring Autumn's pleasant weather;
And the moorcock springs, on whirring wings,
    Amang the blooming heather:
Now waving grain, wide o'er the plain,
    Delights the weary farmer;
And the moon shines bright, when I rove at night,
    To muse upon my charmer.

The partridge loves the fruitful fells;
    The plover loves the mountains;
The woodcock haunts the lonely dells;
    The soaring hern the fountains:
Thro' lofty groves, the cushat roves,
    The path of man to shun it;
The hazel bush o'erhangs the thrush,
    The spreading thorn the linnet.

Thus ev'ry kind their pleasure find,
    The savage and the tender;
Some social join, and leagues combine;
    Some solitary wander;
Avaunt, away! the cruel sway,
    Tyrannic man's dominion;
The sportsman's joy, the murd'ring cry,
    The flutt'ring, gory pinion!

But Peggy dear, the ev'ning's clear,
    Thick flies the skimming swallow;
The sky is blue, the fields in view,
    All fading-green and yellow:
Come let us stray our gladsome way,
    And view the charms of nature;

The rustling corn, the fruited thorn,
  And ev'ry happy creature.

We'll gently walk, and sweetly talk,
  Till the silent moon shine clearly;
I'll grasp thy waist, and fondly prest,
  Swear how I love thee dearly:
Not vernal show'rs to budding flow'rs,
  Not autumn to the farmer,
So dear can be, as thou to me,
  My fair, my lovely charmer!

                                        Robert Burns

Three Years in Glen Garry

Three years' accounts from gamekeepers' records, an estate
kept for seasonal deer-stalking, all manner of Game preservation.
The statistics are false only in that the categories are derived
from dialect, gaelic names for fauna; they are not stories
    contrived . . .
Three hundred and seventy-one rough-legged buzzards (both
    Buteos?)
Two hundred and seventy-five 'Kitehawks'; which might,
    ought,
to have included unknown amounts of various 'shitehawks'.
Two hundred and forty-six martens, precious today our marten
One hundred and ninety-eight wild cats, a hundred and six
    polecats
– the one much reduced but recovering, the other yet to come
    back from the feral.
Ninety-eight peregrine falcons, six even of the Arctic gyr-falcons
seventy-eight merlins, no kestrels? (further, seven 'orange-legged'
    falcons)

sixty-three harriers, probably mainly hen-harriers. Ditto
goshawks.
Thirty-five 'horned' owls (the 'eared' species of owls, *incertae
sedis*)
twenty-seven 'white-tailed' eagles (some the young, fifteen
golden eagles)
eighteen ospreys, eleven hobbies; which might be average say for
today.
The Clearances were not only of the people, but of most of the
other indigenes
at their climax; their dynamic climax, proliferating genes
culminating food-chains, being the noblest, most beautiful, most
evolved.
A country that was ours to inherit, and theirs, gone under oxters'
sweep.
'Garry, stretch thy bare limbs in sleep; it gars me sair to see ye
weep.'

Colin Simms

Lapwing

Two Pewits

Under the after-sunset sky
Two pewits sport and cry,
More white than is the moon on high
Riding the dark surge silently;
More black than earth. Their cry
Is the one sound under the sky.
They alone move, now low, now high,
And merrily they cry
To the mischievous Spring sky,
Plunging earthward, tossing high,
Over the ghost who wonders why
So merrily they cry and fly,
Nor choose 'twixt earth and sky,
While the moon's quarter silently
Rides, and earth rests as silently.

Edward Thomas

Plovers

The plovers come down hard, then clear again,
for they are the embodiment of rain.

Paul Muldoon

Sandpiper

Sandpiper

The roaring alongside he takes for granted,
and that every so often the world is bound to shake.
He runs, he runs to the south, finical, awkward,
in a state of controlled panic, a student of Blake.

The beach hisses like fat. On his left, a sheet
of interrupting water comes and goes
and glazes over his dark and brittle feet.
He runs, he runs straight through it, watching his toes.

– Watching, rather, the spaces of sand between them,
where (no detail too small) the Atlantic drains
rapidly backwards and downwards. As he runs,
he stares at the dragging grains.

The world is a mist. And then the world is
minute and vast and clear. The tide
is higher or lower. He couldn't tell you which.
His beak is focussed; he is preoccupied,

looking for something, something, something.
Poor bird, he is obsessed!
The millions of grains are black, white, tan, and gray,
mixed with quartz grains, rose and amethyst.

Elizabeth Bishop

Curlew

Curlew

She dips her bill in the rim of the sea.
Her beak is the ellipse
of a world much smaller
than that far section of the sea's
circumference. A curve enough to calculate
the field's circle and its heart
of eggs in the cold grass.

All day while I scythed my territory
out of nettles, laid claim to my cantref,
she has cut her share of sky. Her song bubbles
long as a plane trail from her savage mouth.
I clean the blade with newspaper. Dusk blurs
circle within circle till there's nothing left
but the egg pulsing in the dark against her ribs.
For each of us the possessed space contracts
to the nest's heat, the blood's small circuit.

Gillian Clarke

Greenshank

Greenshank

His single note – one can't help calling it
piping, one can't help
calling it plaintive – slides droopingly down
no more than a semitone, but is filled
with an octave of loneliness, with the whole sad scale
of desolation.

He won't leave us. He keeps flying
fifty yards and perching
on a rock or a small hummock,
drawing attention to himself.
Then he calls and calls
and flies on again
in a flight
roundshouldered but dashing,
skulking yet bold.

Cuckoo, phoenix, nightingale,
you are no truer emblems
than this bird is.
He is the melancholy that flies
in the weathers of my mind,
He is the loneliness that calls to me there
in a semitone
of desolate octaves.

Norman MacCaig

Snipe

To the Snipe

Lover of swamps
The quagmire overgrown
With hassock tufts of sedge – where fear encamps
Around thy home alone

The trembling grass
Quakes from the human foot
Nor bears the weight of man to let him pass
Where thou alone and mute

Sittest at rest
In safety neath the clump
Of hugh flag-forrest that thy haunts invest
Or some old sallow stump

Thriving on seams
That tiny islands swell
Just hilling from the mud and rancid streams
Suiting thy nature well

For here thy bill
Suited by wisdom good
Of rude unseemly length doth delve and drill
The gelid mass for food

And here may hap
When summer suns hath dressed
The moors rude desolate and spungy lap
May hide thy mystic nest

Mystic indeed
For isles that ocean make
Are scarcely more secure for birds to build
Than this flag-hidden lake

Boys thread the woods
To their remotest shades,
But in these marshy flats these stagnant floods
Security pervades

From year to year
Places untrodden lie
Where man nor boy nor stock hath ventured near
– Nought gazed on but the sky

And fowl that dread
The very breath of man
Hiding in spots that never knew his tread
A wild and timid clan

Wigeon and teal
And wild duck – restless lot
That from mans dreaded sight will ever steal
To the most dreary spot

Here tempests howl
Around each flaggy plot
Where they who dread mans sight the waterfowl
Hide and are frighted not

Tis power divine
That heartens them to brave
The roughest tempest and at ease recline
On marshes or the wave

Yet instinct knows
Not safetys bounds to shun
The firmer ground where stalking fowler goes
With searching dogs and gun

By tepid springs
Scarcely one stride across
Though brambles from its edge a shelter flings
Thy safety is at loss

And never chuse
The little sinky foss
Streaking the moores whence spa-red water spews
From puddles fringed with moss

Free booters there
Intent to kill or slay
Startle with cracking guns the trepid air
And dogs thy haunts betray.

From dangers reach
Here thou art safe to roam
Far as these washy flag-sown marshes stretch
A still and quiet home

In these thy haunts
Ive gleaned habitual love
From the vague world where pride and folly taunts
I muse and look above

Thy solitudes
The unbounded heaven esteems
And here my heart warms into higher moods
And dignifying dreams

I see the sky
Smile on the meanest spot
Giving to all that creep or walk or fly
A calm and cordial lot

Thine teaches me
Right feelings to employ
That in the dreariest places peace will be
A dweller and a joy

                                            John Clare

The Backward Look

A stagger in air
as if a language
failed, a sleight
of wing.

A snipe's bleat is fleeing
its nesting ground
into dialect,
into variants,

transliterations whirr
on the nature reserves —
little goat of the air,
of the evening,

little goat of the frost.
It is his tail-feathers
drumming elegies
in the slipstream

of wild goose
and yellow bittern
as he corkscrews away
into the vaults

that we live off, his flight
through the sniper's eyrie,
over twilit earthworks
and wall-steads,

disappearing among
gleanings and leavings
in the combs
of a fieldworker's archive.

Seamus Heaney

Kittiwake

At Marsden Bay

Arid hot desert stretched here in the early
Permian Period – sand dune fossils
are pressed to a brownish bottom stratum.
A tropical saline ocean next silted
calcium and magnesium carbonates
over this bed, forming rough Magnesian
Limestone cliffs on the ledges of which
Rissa tridactyla colonises –
an estimated four thousand pairs
that shuttle like close-packed tracer bullets
against dark sky between nests and North Sea.
The call is a shrill 'kit-e-wayke, kit-e-wayke',
also a low 'uk-uk-uk' and a plaintive
'ee-e-e-eeh, ee-e-e-eeh'.

Four boys about sixteen years old appear
in Army Stores combat jackets, one wearing
a balaclava with long narrow eye-slit
(such as a rapist might find advantageous),
bleached denims rolled up to mid-calf, tall laced boots
with bright polished toe-caps, pates cropped to stubble.
Three of the four are cross-eyed, all are acned.
Communication consists of bellowing
simian ululations between

each other at only a few inches range:
'Gibbo, gerroffforal getcher yaffuga',
also a low 'lookadembastabirdsmon'.

Gibbo grubs up a Magnesian Limestone
chunk and assails the ledges at random,
biffing an incubating kittiwake
full in the sternum – an audible slap.
Wings bent the wrong way, it thumps at the cliffbase,
twitching, half closing an eye. Gibbo seizes
a black webbed foot and swings the lump joyously
round and round his head. It emits
a strange wheezing noise. Gibbo's pustular pal
is smacked in the face by the flung poultry, yowls,
and lobs it out into the foam. The four
gambol euphoric like drunk chimps through rock pools.
Nests are dislodged, brown-blotched shells crepitate
exuding thick rich orange embryo goo
under a hail of hurled fossilised desert
two hundred and eighty million years old.

Peter Reading

Dodo

Ye haue heard this yarn afore

(but I'm minded on it againe
thefe daies of fqualls and rank clouds
and raines as is uitriolic –
pines fhorn ftark as mizzen-mafts
wi neuer a frolicfome fowl –
and ye top-gallant air all rent):

how we was one Monday anchored
off Mafcarenhas Iflande
in fourteen fathom o water;
how, feeking diuerfion, we landed;
how, on ye trees, there was pigeons
as blue as polifhed flate
which fuffered vs, being fo tame,
for to pluck em iuft like fruits
from ye branches and pull their necks;
how we killed two hundred firft day;
how we alfo killed grey paraquets
(moft entertayninge to cetch
a grey paraquet and *twift* it
fo as it fqueals aloud
till ye reft of its kind flock round,
therevpon themfelues being cetched);
how there was alfo penguins
(which laft hath but ftumps for wings,
fo being ye eafier to kill)

which we killed above four hundred;
how there was alfo wild geefe
and turtles above an hundred;
how we killed all thefe and more;
and ye Tuefday more and more;
and ye Wednefday more and more;
and ye Thurfday more and more;
ye haue heard this yarn afore.

Peter Reading

Rock Dove/Feral Pigeon

'I had a dove and the sweet dove died'

I had a dove and the sweet dove died,
   And I have thought it died of grieving.
Oh, what could it grieve for? Its feet were tied
   With a silken thread of my own hand's weaving.
Sweet little red feet! Why should you die –
Why would you leave me, sweet dove! Why?
You lived alone on the forest-tree,
Why, pretty thing, could you not live with me?
I kissed you oft and gave you white peas;
Why not live sweetly, as in the green trees?

John Keats

Pigeons

Older than the ancient Greeks, than
Solomon, the pigeon family is a
ramifying one, a
banyan of banyans; to begin
with, bluish slate,
   but with ability. Modesty cannot dull
   the lustre of the pigeon
   swift and sure, coming quickest and
straightest just after a storm. The great

lame war hero Cher Ami, the
Lost Battalion's gallant bird; and
Mocker with one eye
    destroyed, delivering his despatch
to his superiors; and Sergeant Dunn,
civilian pigeon who flew eight
hundred sixty-eight miles
in four days and six hours;
    and destined to hatch
in France, Spike, veteran of
the division in which Mocker
    served – exceptional messenger,
'Rarely was confidence misplaced' a newspaper
says. Dastardly comment
    inexactly phrased, as used of Her-
mes, Ariel, or Leander –
pigeons of the past. Neither was confidence
misplaced in the Javan-
Sumatran birds the Dutch had had
brought from Baghdad.
Mysterious animal with a magnetic
feel by which he traces back-
    ward his transportation outward,
even in a fog at sea, though glad
    to be tossed near enough the loft
    or coop to get back the same day.
'Home on time without
    his message.' What matter since he has
got back. Migrating always in the same
direction, bringing all letters
to the same address, see-
ing better homes than his,
    he is not Theudas
boasting himself to be some-
body, this anonymous post-
    man who, as soon as he could fly,

was carrying valentines and messages of
state; or soberer news –
   'So please write me and believe that I
am yours very truly;' fine words
those. An instrument, not just an instinctive
individual, this
dove, that lifts his right foot over
the alighting-
   board to rejoin his ungainly pin-clad dark-skinned
brood as domestic turtle-
doves might; two. Invariably
two. The turtle, a not exciting
bird – in Britain shy, detected
by its constantly heard coo, with-
out a song but not
   without a voice – does well to stay far
out of sight; but the Pelew pigeon with
black head, metallic wasp-lustred
grass-green breast and purple
legs and feet, need not; nor
   need the Nicobar,
novel, narrow-feathered dove.

Marianne Moore

Pigeons

On shallow slates the pigeons shift together,
Backing against a thin rain from the west
Blown across each sunk head and settled feather.
Huddling round the warm stack suits them best,
Till winter daylight weakens, and they grow
Hardly defined against the brickwork. Soon,
Light from a small intense lopsided moon
Shows them, black as their shadows, sleeping so.

Philip Larkin

Pigeons at Dawn

Extraordinary efforts are being made
To hide things from us, my friend.
Some stay up into the wee hours
To search their souls.
Others undress each other in darkened rooms.

The creaky old elevator
Took us down to the icy cellar first
To show us a mop and a bucket
Before it deigned to ascend again
With a sigh of exasperation.

Under the vast, early dawn sky
The city lay silent before us.
Everything on hold:
Rooftops and water towers,
Clouds and wisps of white smoke.

We must be patient, we told ourselves,
See if the pigeons will coo now
For the one who comes to her window
To feed them angel cake,
All but invisible, but for her slender arm.

Charles Simic

Wood Pigeon

Wood-Pigeons

The army chap says –
to get conversation flowing –
'Women are more adapted to life
than men. They get less hurt.
Keep more of themselves back.'

His wife of thirty years,
a bony, brainy woman
with pale, frizzy curls and
baby-blue eyes, gently remonstrates.
The others join in –

chuckling, smoothing,
while trying to wrestle
with small tough parcels
that sit in red pools of sauce
on each blue-patterned plate.

In the end, the hostess
has to raid the kitchen drawer
for the sharpest knives
so her guests can dismember
the wood-pigeons.

In her silver-beaded dress
she looks like the knife-thrower's girl
at the circus – carvers
bunched in her hands
like dangerous flowers.

Vicki Feaver

Orange Dove

The Orange Dove of Fiji

To R. and B. O'H

On the slopes of Taveuni
The Barking Pigeons woof
But when I saw the Orange Dove
I nearly hit the roof

And would have surely had there been
A roof around to hit
But the roofs of Taveuni
Are down on the lower bit

While up there in the forest
The Silktails have survived
And they 'forage in the substage'
And you feel you have *arrived*

As an amateur ornithologist
In the midst of a Silktail flock
Until you hear behind you
A 'penetrating tock'

And you find six feet above your head
What you were looking for –
The Orange Dove of Fiji,
No less, no more.

The female of the Orange Dove
Is actually green.
The really orange *male* Orange Dove
Is the one you've seen.

It must have been dipped in Dayglo
Held by its bright green head.
The colour is preposterous.
You want to drop down dead.

It turns around upon its perch
Displaying all the bits
That are mentioned in Dick Watling's book
And the description fits.

Then it says: 'Tock – okay, is that
Enough to convince you yet?
Because that, my friend, is all tock tock
That you are going to get.'

Oh, the Many-Coloured Fruit Dove
Is pretty enough to boot
And I'm afraid the Purple Swamphen
Looks queerer than a coot

Like a flagrant English Bishop
Let loose among his flock
With brand-new orange gaiters
(And that's just the Swamphen cock.)

But the Orange Dove is something
Spectacular to see.
So I hope they don't fell another single
Taveuni tree.

James Fenton

NOTE: Watling, *Birds of Fiji, Tonga and Samoa*, Croom, Helm, 1982

Emerald Dove

The Emerald Dove

We ought to hang cutout hawk shapes
in our windows. Birds hard driven
by a predator, or maddened by a mirrored rival
too often die zonk against the panes'
invisible sheer, or stagger away from
the blind full stop in the air.
It was different with the emerald dove.
In at an open sash, a pair

sheered, missile, in a punch of energy,
one jinking on through farther doors, one
thrown, panicked by that rectangular wrong copse, braked
like a bullet in blood, a full-on splat of wings
like a vaulter between shoulders, blazed and calliper,
ashriek out of jagbeaked fixed fury, swatting wind,
lights, keepsakes, panes, then at the in window out, gone.
A sparrowhawk, by the cirrus feathering.

The other, tracked down in a farther room
clinging to a bedhead, was the emerald dove,
a rainforest bird, flashed in beyond its world
of lice, sudden death and tree seeds. Pigeon-like,

only its eye and neck in liquid motion,
there, as much beyond us as beyond
itself, it perched, barefoot in silks
like a prince of Sukhothai, above the reading lamps and
     cotton-buds.

Modest-sized as a writing hand, mushroom fawn
apart from its paua casque, those viridescent closed wings,
it was an emerald Levite in that bedroom
which the memory of it was going to bless for years
despite topping our ordinary happiness, as beauty
makes background of all around it. Levite too
in the question it posed: sanctuary without transformation,
which is, how we might be,

plunged out of our contentment into evolved strange heaven,
where the need to own or mate with or eat the beautiful
was bygone as poverty,
and we were incomprehensibly, in our exhaustion,
treasured, cooed at, then softly left alone
among vast crumples, verticals, refracting air,
our way home barred by mirrors, our splendour unmanifest
to us now, a small wild person, with no idea of peace.

                                        Les Murray

Collared Dove

Listening to Collared Doves

I am homesick now for middle age, as then
For youth. For youth is our home-land: we were born
And lived there long, though afterwards moved on
From state to state, too slowly acclimatising
Perhaps and never fluent, through the surprising
Countries, in any languages but one.

This mourning now for middle age, no more
For youth, confirms me old as not before.
Age rounds the world, they say, to childhood's far
Archaic shores; it may be so at last.
But what now (strength apart) I miss the most
Is time unseen like air, since everywhere.

And yet, when in the months and in the skies
That were the cuckoos', and in the nearer trees
That were the deep-voiced wood-pigeons', it is
Instead now the collared doves that call and call
(Their three flat notes growing traditional),
I think we live long enough, listening to these.

I draw my line out from their simple curve
And say, our natural span may be enough;
And think of one I knew and her long life;
And how the climate changed and how the sign-
Posts changed, defaced, from her Victorian
Childhood and youth, through our century of grief;

And how she adapted as she could, not one
By nature adaptable, bred puritan
(Though quick to be pleased and having still her own
Lightness of heart). She died twenty years ago,
Aged, of life – it seems, all she could do
Having done, all the change that she could know
    having known.

                                        E. J. Scovell

Parrot

Parrot

The old sick green parrot
High in a dingy cage
Sick with malevolent rage
Beadily glutted his furious eye
On the old dark
Chimneys of Noel Park

Far from his jungle green
Over the seas he came
To the yellow skies, to the dripping rain,
To the night of his despair.
And the pavements of his street
Are shining beneath the lamp
With a beauty that's not for one
Born under a tropic sun.

He has croup. His feathered chest
Knows no minute of rest.
High on his perch he sits
And coughs and spits,
Waiting for death to come.
Pray heaven it wont be long.

Stevie Smith

Parakeet

Bird Lady

Under a pine in Vondelpark
the Bird Lady has fashioned
an impromptu feed-table,
arrives each morning laden
with bags of sunflower seeds
and kibbled maize and proceeds
to feed the feral Rose-rings
(*Psittacula krameri*,
40 centimetres,
general plumage green,
yellowish underwing,
in male, rose collar encircling
hindneck, nape suffused
bluish) and Alexandrines
(*Psittacula eupatria*,
58 centimetres,
a group of pristine males,
occiput and cheeks
suffused with bluish-grey,
black stripe through lower cheek,
pink collar encircling hindneck,
red slash on secondary coverts,
massive vermilion bill,
call – a skreeching *kee-ak*),
which, were it not for her

genial dottiness,
would not survive the severe
calorie-wasting winter,
and *we* would be undernourished.

Peter Reading

A Day Out 3

Autumn Birds

The wild duck startles like a sudden thought
And heron slow as if it might be caught
The flopping crows on weary wing go bye
And grey beard jackdaws noising as they flye
The crowds of starnels wiz and hurry bye
And darken like a cloud the evening sky
The larks like thunder rise and suthy round
Then drop and nestle in the stubble ground
The wild swan hurrys high and noises loud
With white necks peering to the evening cloud
The weary rooks to distant woods are gone
With length of tail the magpie winnows on
To neighbouring tree and leaves the distant crow
While small birds nestle in the hedge below

John Clare

Bird Study

A worm writhes and you have some power
Of knowing when and where to strike.
Then suddenly bread in a shower.
Being a bird is like

This and a feathered overcoat,
A throb of sound, a balanced wing,
A quiver of the beak and throat,
A gossip-mongering.

But higher up a hawk will take
Stature of stars, a comet-fall,
Or else a swan that oars a lake,
Or one note could be all.

I am obsessed with energy
I never touch. I am alive
To what I only hear and see,
The sweep, the sharp, the drive.

Elizabeth Jennings

'Then we waded at low tide'

Then we waded at low tide to Hilbre Island;/and we marvelled at
scores of thousands of waders – / Sanderling, Knot, Oystercatcher,
Redshank, Curlew and Dunlin;/and the giant gull of the north, the
hyperborean Glaucous,/glided snow-mantled above the remains of
the old lifeboat station;/and there suddenly stooped from a cloud
the colour of Blaenau Ffestiniog slate/a Peregrine into a blizzard
of wheeling *Calidris alba*/and the falcon hit and we heard the thud
and a handful of silvern feathers/whorled in the wind and the great
dark raptor rose with the dead meat locked in its talons;/and I said
to my friend: 'We will mind this as long as we live.' (He is dead
now.)

Peter Reading

Initial Illumination

Farne cormorants with catches in their beaks
shower fishscale confetti on the shining sea.
The first bright weather here for many weeks
for my Sunday G-Day train bound for Dundee,
off to St Andrew's to record a reading,
doubtful, in these dark days, what poems can do,
and watching the mists round Lindisfarne receding
my doubt extends to Dark Age Good Book too.
Eadfrith the Saxon scribe/illuminator
incorporated cormorants I'm seeing fly
round the same island thirteen centuries later
into the *In principio*'s initial I.
Billfrith's begemmed and jewelled boards get looted
by raiders gung-ho for booty and berserk,
the sort of soldiery that's still recruited
to do today's dictators' dirty work,
but the initials in St John and in St Mark
graced with local cormorants in ages,
we of a darker still keep calling Dark,
survive in those illuminated pages.
The word of God so beautifully scripted
by Eadfrith and Billfrith the anchorite
Pentagon conners have once again conscripted
to gloss the cross on the precision sight.
Candlepower, steady hand, gold leaf, a brush
were all that Eadfrith had to beautify
the word of God much bandied by George Bush
whose word illuminated midnight sky
and confused the Baghdad cock who was betrayed
by bombs into believing day was dawning
and crowed his heart out at the deadly raid
and didn't live to greet the proper morning.
Now with noonday headlights in Kuwait

and the burial of the blackened in Baghdad
let them remember, all those who celebrate,
that their good news is someone else's bad
or the light will never dawn on poor Mankind.
Is it open-armed at all that victory V,
that insular initial intertwined
with slack-necked cormorants from black laquered sea,
with trumpets bulled and bellicose and blowing
for what men claim as victories in their wars,
with the fire-hailing cock and all those crowing
who don't yet smell the dunghill at their claws?

Tony Harrison

Bird Walk

White nights feather my mind.
I am a giant of sleeplessness, as high
as the cliff where auks lay teetering eggs
which droop roughly, like tears.

They won't roll. My mind rolls.
To sleep, I must think like the birds
in camouflage, decoys and patrols.

Redshanks storm the grass, post sentries
on telegraph poles, as highly strung
as the oystercatchers all in a flap,
outcrying their young to mislead crows
who shrug and brag and lunge.

At three a.m., a black cormorant dives.
A needle, a nightfall, it closes my eyes.

Lavinia Greenlaw

Cuckoo

Cuckoo

Sumer is icumen in,
Loud sing cuckoo!
Groweth seed and bloweth mead
And springeth the wood now.
Sing cuckoo!

Ewe bleateth after lamb,
Cow loweth after calf,
Bullock starteth, buck farteth,
Merry sing cuckoo!

Cuckoo, cuckoo!
Well singest thou cuckoo,
Nor cease thou never now!

Sing cuckoo now, sing cuckoo!
Sing cuckoo, sing cuckoo now!

Anonymous

The Cuckoo

O the cuckoo she's a pretty bird,
   She singeth as she flies,
She bringeth good tidings,
   She telleth no lies.

She sucketh white flowers
   For to keep her voice clear,
And the more she singeth cuckoo
   The summer draweth near.

Anonymous

To the Cuckoo

O blithe new-comer! I have heard,
I hear thee and rejoice.
O cuckoo! shall I call thee bird,
Or but a wandering voice?

While I am lying on the grass
Thy twofold shout I hear,
From hill to hill it seems to pass
At once far off, and near.

Though babbling only to the vale,
Of sunshine and of flowers,
Thou bringest unto me a tale
Of visionary hours.

Thrice welcome, darling of the spring!
Even yet thou art to me
No bird, but an invisible thing,
A voice, a mystery;

The same whom in my schoolboy days
I listened to; that cry
Which made me look a thousand ways
In bush, and tree, and sky.

To seek thee did I often rove
Through woods and on the green;
And thou wert still a hope, a love;
Still longed for, never seen.

And I can listen to thee yet;
Can lie upon the plain
And listen, till I do beget
That golden time again.

O blessëd bird! the earth we pace
Again appears to be
An unsubstantial, faery place;
That is fit home for thee!

                                William Wordsworth

'Repeat that, repeat'

Repeat that, repeat,
Cuckoo, bird, and open ear wells, heart-springs, delightfully sweet,
With a ballad, with a ballad, a rebound
Off trundled timber and scoops of the hillside ground, hollow
    hollow hollow ground:
The whole landscape flushes on a sudden at a sound.

                                        Gerard Manley Hopkins

Short Ode to the Cuckoo

No one now imagines you answer idle questions
– *How long shall I live? How long remain single?*
Will butter be cheaper? – nor does your shout make
    husbands uneasy.

Compared with arias by the great performers
such as the merle, your two-note act is kid-stuff:
our most hardened crooks are sincerely shocked by
    your nesting habits.

Science, Aesthetics, Ethics, may huff and puff but they
cannot extinguish your magic: you marvel
the commuter as you wondered the savage.
    Hence, in my diary,

where I normally enter nothing but social
engagements and, lately, the death of friends, I
scribble year after year when I first hear you,
    of a holy moment.

                                        W. H. Auden

Tawny Owl

'Sweet Suffolk owl'

Sweet Suffolk owl, so trimly dight
With feathers like a lady bright,
Thou sing'st alone, sitting by night,
   Te whit, te whoo, te whit, te whoo.
Thy note, that forth so freely rolls,
With shrill command the mouse controls,
And sings a dirge for dying souls,
   Te whit, te whoo, te whit, te whoo.

Anonymous

Barn Owl

Barn Owl

1

Mostly it is a pale
face hovering in the afterdraught
of the spirit, making both ends meet
on a scream. It is the breath
of the churchyard, the forming
of white frost in a believer,
when he would pray; it is soft
feathers camouflaging a machine.

It repeats itself year
after year in its offspring,
the staring pupils it teaches
its music to, that is the voice
of God in the darkness cursing himself
fiercely for his lack of love.

2

and there the owl happens
like white frost as
cruel and as silent
and the time on its
blank face is not
now so the dead
have nothing to go

by and are fast
or slow but never punctual
as the alarm is
over their bleached bones
of its night-strangled cry.

R. S. Thomas

Nightjar

The Fern Owls Nest

The weary woodman rocking home beneath
His tightly banded faggot wonders oft
While crossing over the furze crowded heath
To hear the fern owls cry that whews aloft
In circling whirls and often by his head
Whizzes as quick as thought and ill at rest,
As through the rustling ling with heavy tread
He goes nor heeds he tramples near its nest
That underneath the furze or squatting thorn
Lies hidden on the ground and teazing round
That lonely spot she wakes her jarring noise
To the unheeding waste till mottled morn
Fills the red east with daylights coming sound
And the heaths echoes mock the herding boys

John Clare

The Dor-Hawk

Fern-owl, Churn-owl, or Goat-sucker,
   Night-jar, Dor-hawk, or whate'er
Be thy name among a dozen, –
Whip-poor-Will's and Who-are-you's cousin,
Chuck-Will's-widow's near relation,
Thou art at thy night vocation,
   Thrilling the still evening air!

In the dark brown wood beyond us,
   Where the night lies dusk and deep;
Where the fox his burrow maketh,
Where the tawny owl awaketh
   Nightly from his day-long sleep;

There Dor-hawk is thy abiding,
   Meadow green is not for thee;
While the aspen branches shiver,
'Mid the roaring of the river,
   Comes thy chirring voice to me.

Bird, thy form I never looked on,
   And to see it do not care;
Thou has been, and thou art only
As a voice of forests lonely,
   Heard and dwelling only there.

Mary Howitt

Whippoorwill

In Midsummer Quiet

Ariadne's bird,
That lone
Whippoorwill.

Ball of twilight thread
Unraveling furtively.
Tawny thread,
Raw, pink the thread end.

A claw or two also
To pare, snip . . .
After which it sits still
For the stream to explain why it shivers

So.
    Resuming, farther on,
Intermittently,
By the barn
Where the first stars are –
In quotation marks,
As it were – O phantom

Bird!
Dreaming of my own puzzles
And mazes.

                                        Charles Simic

Swift

The Swifts

How at once should I know,
When stretched in the harvest blue
I saw the swift's black bow,
That I would not have that view
Another day
Until next May
Again it is due?

The same year after year –
But with the swift alone.
With other things I but fear
That they will be over and done
Suddenly
And I only see
Them to know them gone.

Edward Thomas

Swifts

Fifteenth of May. Cherry blossom. The swifts
Materialise at the tip of a long scream
Of needle. 'Look! They're back! Look!' And they're gone
On a steep

Controlled scream of skid
Round the house-end and away under the cherries. Gone.
Suddenly flickering in sky summit, three or four together,
Gnat-whisp frail, and hover-searching, and listening

For air-chills – are they too early? With a bowing
Power-thrust to left, then to right, then a flicker they
Tilt into a slide, a tremble for balance,
Then a lashing down disappearance

Behind elms.
                    They've made it again,
Which means the globe's still working, the Creation's
Still waking refreshed, our summer's
Still all to come –
                    And here they are, here they are again
Erupting across yard stones
Shrapnel-scatter terror. Frog-gapers,
Speedway goggles, international mobsters –

A bolas of three or four wire screams
Jockeying across each other
On their switchback wheel of death.
They swat past, hard-fletched,

Veer on the hard air, toss up over the roof,
And are gone again. Their mole-dark labouring,
Their lunatic limber scramming frenzy
And their whirling blades

Sparkle out into blue –
                    Not ours any more.
Rats ransacked their nests so now they shun us.
Round luckier houses now
They crowd their evening dirt-track meetings,

Racing their discords, screaming as if speed-burned,
Head-height, clipping the doorway
With their leaden velocity and their butterfly lightness,
Their too much power, their arrow-thwack into the eaves.

Every year a first-fling, nearly-flying
Misfit flopped in our yard,
Groggily somersaulting to get airborne.
He bat-crawled on his tiny useless feet, tangling his flails

Like a broken toy, and shrieking thinly
Till I tossed him up – then suddenly he flowed away under
His bowed shoulders of enormous swimming power,
Slid away along levels wobbling

On the fine wire they have reduced life to,
And crashed among the raspberries.
Then followed fiery hospital hours
In a kitchen. The moustached goblin savage

Nested in a scarf. The bright blank
Blind, like an angel, to my meat-crumbs and flies.
Then eyelids resting. Wasted clingers curled.
The inevitable balsa death.

                    Finally burial
For the husk
Of my little Apollo –

The charred scream
Folded in its huge power.

                                        Ted Hughes

Hummingbird

Humming-Bird

I can imagine, in some otherworld
Primeval-dumb, far back
In that most awful stillness, that only gasped and hummed,
Humming-birds raced down the avenues.

Before anything had a soul,
While life was a heave of Matter, half inanimate,
This little bit chipped off in brilliance
And went whizzing through the slow, vast, succulent stems.

I believe there were no flowers, then,
In the world where the humming-bird flashed ahead of
　　creation.
I believe he pierced the slow vegetable veins with his long
　　beak.

Probably he was big
As mosses, and little lizards, they say were once big.
Probably he was a jabbing, terrifying monster.

We look at him through the wrong end of the long telescope of
　　Time,
Luckily for us.

　　　　　　　　　　　　　　　　　　D. H. Lawrence

Deaths & Depletions 3

'Dead in the cold'

Dead in the cold, a song-singing thrush,
Dead at the foot of a snowberry bush, –
Weave him a coffin of rush,
Dig him a grave where the soft mosses grow,
Raise him a tombstone of snow.

Christina Rossetti

The Selfsame Song

A bird sings the selfsame song,
With never a fault in its flow,
That we listened to here those long
    Long years ago.

A pleasing marvel is how
A strain of such rapturous rote
Should have gone on thus till now
    Unchanged in a note!

– But it's not the selfsame bird. –
No: perished to dust is he . . .
As also are those who heard
    That song with me.

Thomas Hardy

February Afternoon

Men heard this roar of parleying starlings, saw,
A thousand years ago even as now,
Black rooks with white gulls following the plough
So that the first are last until a caw
Commands that last are first again, – a law
Which was of old when one, like me, dreamed how
A thousand years might dust lie on his brow
Yet thus would birds do between hedge and shaw.

Time swims before me, making as a day
A thousand years, while the broad ploughland oak
Roars mill-like and men strike and bear the stroke
Of war as ever, audacious or resigned,
And God still sits aloft in the array
That we have wrought him, stone-deaf and stone-blind.

Edward Thomas

Hurt Hawks

I

The broken pillar of the wing jags from the clotted shoulder,
The wing trails like a banner in defeat,
No more to use the sky forever but live with famine
And pain a few days: cat nor coyote
Will shorten the week of waiting for death, there is game
    without talons.
He stands under the oak-bush and waits
The lame feet of salvation; at night he remembers freedom
And flies in a dream, the dawns ruin it.

He is strong and pain is worse to the strong, incapacity is
    worse.
The curs of the day come and torment him
At distance, no one but death the redeemer will humble that
    head,
The intrepid readiness, the terrible eyes.
The wild God of the world is sometimes merciful to those
That ask mercy, not often to the arrogant.
You do not know him, you communal people, or you have
    forgotten him;
Intemperate and savage, the hawk remembers him;
Beautiful and wild, the hawks, and men that are dying,
    remember him.

II

I'd sooner, except the penalties, kill a man than a hawk; but
    the great redtail
Had nothing left but unable misery
From the bone too shattered for mending, the wing that
    trailed under his talons when he moved.
We had fed him six weeks, I gave him freedom,
He wandered over the foreland hill and returned in the
    evening, asking for death,
Not like a beggar, still eyed with the old
Implacable arrogance. I gave him the lead gift in the twilight.
    What fell was relaxed,
Owl-downy, soft feminine feathers; but what
Soared: the fierce rush: the night-herons by the flooded river
    cried fear at its rising
Before it was quite unsheathed from reality.

                                    Robinson Jeffers

Neighbours

That spring was late. We watched the sky
and studied charts for shouldering isobars.
Birds were late to pair. Crows drank from the lamb's eye.

Over Finland small birds fell: song-thrushes
steering north, smudged signatures on light,
migrating warblers, nightingales.

Wing-beats failed over fjords, each lung a sip of gall.
Children were warned of their dangerous beauty.
Milk was spilt in Poland. Each quarrel

the blowback from some old story,
a mouthful of bitter air from the Ukraine
brought by the wind out of its box of sorrows.

This spring a lamb sips caesium on a Welsh hill.
A child, lifting her face to drink the rain,
takes into her blood the poisoned arrow.

Now we are all neighbourly, each little town
in Europe twinned to Chernobyl, each heart
with the burnt fireman, the child on the Moscow train.

In the democracy of the virus and the toxin
we wait. We watch for bird migrations,
one bird returning with green in its voice,

glasnost,
golau glas,
a first break of blue.

Gillian Clarke

NOTE: *golau glas*: blue light

Kingfisher

The Kingfisher

It was the Rainbow gave thee birth,
And left thee all her lovely hues;
    And, as her mother's name was Tears,
So runs it in my blood to choose
    For haunts the lonely pools, and keep
    In company with trees that weep.

    Go you and, with such glorious hues,
Live with proud peacocks in green parks;
    On lawns as smooth as shining glass,
Let every feather show its marks;
    Get thee on boughs and clap thy wings
    Before the windows of proud kings.

    Nay, lovely Bird, thou art not vain;
Thou hast no proud, ambitious mind;
    I also love a quiet place
That's green, away from all mankind;
    A lonely pool, and let a tree
    Sigh with her bosom over me.

W. H. Davies

Kingfisher

December took us where the idling water
Rose in a ghost of smoke, its banks hard-thatched
With blanching reeds, the sun in a far quarter.

Short days had struck a bitter chain together
In links of blue and white so closely matched
They made an equipoise we called the weather.

There, the first snowfall grew to carapace,
The pulse beneath it beating slow and blind,
And every kind of absence marked the face

On which we walked as if we were not lost,
As if there was a something there to find
Beneath a sleep of branches grey with frost.

We smiled, and spoke small words which had no hold
Upon the darkness we had carried there,
Our bents and winter dead-things, wisps of cold.

And then, from wastes of stub and nothing came
The Kingfisher, whose instancy laid bare
His proof that ice and sapphire conjure flame.

                                        Peter Scupham

Green Woodpecker

The Green Woodpecker's Nest

The green woodpecker flying up and down
With wings of mellow green and speckled crown
She bores a hole in trees with crawking noise
And pelted down and often catched by boys
She makes a lither nest of grass and whool
Men fright her oft that go the sticks to pull
Ive up and clumb the trees with hook and pole
And stood on rotten grains to reach the hole
And as I trembled upon fear and doubt
I found the eggs and scarce could get them out
I put them in my hat a tattered crown
And scarcely without breaking brought them down
The eggs are small for such a bird they lay
Five eggs and like the sparrows spotted grey

John Clare

Skylark

The Lark Ascending

He rises and begins to round,
He drops the silver chain of sound,
Of many links without a break,
In chirrup, whistle, slur and shake,
All intervolved and spreading wide,
Like water-dimples down a tide
Where ripple ripple overcurls
And eddy into eddy whirls;
A press of hurried notes that run
So fleet they scarce are more than one,
Yet changeingly the trills repeat
And linger ringing while they fleet,
Sweet to the quick o' the ear, and dear
To her beyond the handmaid ear,
Who sits beside our inner springs,
Too often dry for this he brings,
Which seems the very jet of earth
At sight of sun, her music's mirth,
As up he wings the spiral stair,
A song of light, and pierces air
With fountain ardour, fountain play,
To reach the shining tops of day,
And drink in everything discerned
An ecstasy to music turned,
Impelled by what his happy bill
Disperses; drinking, showering still,

Unthinking save that he may give
His voice the outlet, there to live
Renewed in endless notes of glee,
So thirsty of his voice is he,
For all to hear and all to know
That he is joy, awake, aglow,
The tumult of the heart to hear
Through pureness filtered crystal-clear,
And know the pleasure sprinkled bright
By simple singing of delight,
Shrill, irreflective, unrestrained,
Rapt, ringing, on the jet sustained
Without a break, without a fall,
Sweet-silvery, sheer lyrical,
Perennial, quavering up the chord
Like myriad dews of sunny sward
That trembling into fulness shine,
And sparkle dropping argentine;
Such wooing as the ear receives
From zephyr caught in choric leaves
Of aspens when their chattering net
Is flushed to white with shivers wet;
And such the water-spirit's chime
On mountain heights in morning's prime,
Too freshly sweet to seem excess,
Too animate to need a stress;
But wider over many heads
The starry voice ascending spreads,
Awakening, as it waxes thin,
The best in us to him akin;
And every face to watch him raised
Puts on the light of children praised,
So rich our human pleasure ripes
When sweetness on sincereness pipes,
Though nought be promised from the seas,
But only a soft-ruffling breeze

Sweep glittering on a still content,
Serenity in ravishment.
For singing till his heaven fills,
'Tis love of earth that he instils,
And ever winging up and up,
Our valley is his golden cup,
And he the wine which overflows
To lift us with him as he goes:
The woods and brooks, the sheep and kine,
He is, the hills, the human line,
The meadows green, the fallows brown,
The dreams of labour in the town;
He sings the sap, the quickened veins;
The wedding song of sun and rains
He is, the dance of children, thanks
Of sowers, shout of primrose-banks,
And eye of violets while they breathe;
All these the circling song will wreathe,
And you shall hear the herb and tree,
The better heart of men shall see,
Shall feel celestially, as long
As you crave nothing save the song.

Was never voice of ours could say
Our inmost in the sweetest way,
Like yonder voice aloft, and link
All hearers in the song they drink.
Our wisdom speaks from failing blood,
Our passion is too full in flood,
We want the key of his wild note
Of truthful in a tuneful throat,
The song seraphically free
Of taint of personality,
So pure that it salutes the suns,
The voice of one for millions,

In whom the millions rejoice
For giving their one spirit voice.
Yet men have we, whom we revere,
Now names, and men still housing here,
Whose lives, by many a battle-dint
Defaced, and grinding wheels on flint,
Yield substance, though they sing not, sweet
For song our highest heaven to greet:
Whom heavenly singing gives us new,
Enspheres them brilliant in our blue,
From firmest base to farthest leap,
Because their love of Earth is deep,
And they are warriors in accord
With life to serve, and pass reward,
So touching purest and so heard
In the brain's reflex of yon bird:
Wherefore their soul in me, or mine,
Through self-forgetfulness divine,
In them, that song aloft maintains,
To fill the sky and thrill the plains
With showerings drawn from human stores,
As he to silence nearer soars,
Extends the world at wings and dome,
More spacious making more our home,
Till lost on his aërial rings
In light, and then the fancy sings.

George Meredith

To a Skylark

Hail to thee, blithe Spirit!
  Bird thou never wert,
That from Heaven, or near it,
  Pourest thy full heart
In profuse strains of unpremeditated art.

Higher still and higher
  From the earth thou springest
Like a cloud of fire;
  The blue deep thou wingest,
And singing still dost soar, and soaring ever singest.

In the golden lightning
  Of the sunken sun,
O'er which clouds are bright'ning,
  Thou dost float and run;
Like an unbodied joy whose race is just begun.

The pale purple even
  Melts around thy flight;
Like a star of Heaven,
  In the broad daylight
Thou are unseen, but yet I hear thy shrill delight,

Keen as are the arrows
  Of that silver sphere,
Whose intense lamp narrows
  In the white dawn clear
Until we hardly see – we feel that it is there.

All the earth and air
    With thy voice is loud,
As, when night is bare,
    From one lonely cloud
The moon rains out her beams, and Heaven is
        overflowed.

What thou art we know not;
    What is most like thee?
From rainbow clouds there flow not
    Drops so bright to see
As from thy presence showers a rain of melody.

Like a Poet hidden
    In the light of thought,
Singing hymns unbidden,
    Till the world is wrought
To sympathy with hopes and fears it heeded not:

Like a high-born maiden
    In a palace-tower,
Soothing her love-laden
    Soul in secret hour
With music sweet as love, which overflows her
        bower:

Like a glow-worm golden
    In a dell of dew,
Scattering unbeholden
    Its aëreal hue
Among the flowers and grass, which screen it from
        the view!

Like a rose embowered
    In its own green leaves,
By warm winds deflowered,
    Till the scent it gives
Makes faint with too much sweet those heavy-wingèd
        thieves:

Sound of vernal showers
    On the twinkling grass,
Rain-awakened flowers,
    All that ever was
Joyous, and clear, and fresh, thy music doth surpass:

Teach us, Sprite or Bird,
    What sweet thoughts are thine:
I have never heard
    Praise of love or wine
That panted forth a flood of rapture so divine.

Chorus Hymeneal,
    Or triumphal chant,
Matched with thine would be all
    But an empty vaunt,
A thing wherein we feel there is some hidden want.

What objects are the fountains
    Of thy happy strain?
What fields, or waves, or mountains?
    What shapes of sky or plain?
What love of thine own kind? what ignorance of
        pain?

With thy clear keen joyance
  Languor cannot be:
Shadow of annoyance
  Never came near thee:
Thou lovest – but ne'er knew love's sad satiety.

Waking or asleep,
  Thou of death must deem
Things more true and deep
  Than we mortals dream,
Or how could thy notes flow in such a crystal
    stream?

We look before and after,
  And pine for what is not:
Our sincerest laughter
  With some pain is fraught;
Our sweetest songs are those that tell of saddest
    thought.

Yet if we could scorn
  Hate, and pride, and fear;
If we were things born
  Not to shed a tear,
I know not how thy joy we ever should come near.

Better than all measures
  Of delightful sound,
Better than all treasures
  That in books are found,
Thy skill to poet were, thou scorner of the ground!

Teach me half the gladness
    That thy brain must know,
Such harmonious madness
    From my lips would flow
The world should listen then – as I am listening
    now.

Percy Bysshe Shelley

The Caged Skylark

As a dare-gale skylark scanted in a dull cage
    Man's mounting spirit in his bone-house, mean house,
        dwells –
    That bird beyond the remembering his free fells,
This in drudgery, day-labouring-out life's age.

Though aloft on turf or perch or poor low stage,
    Both sing sometímes the sweetest, sweetest spells,
    Yet both droop deadly sómetimes in their cells
Or wring their barriers in bursts of fear or rage.

Not that the sweet-fowl, song-fowl, needs no rest –
Why, hear him, hear him babble and drop down to his nest,
    But his own nest, wild nest, no prison.

Man's spirit will be flesh-bound when found at best,
But uncumberèd: meadow-down is not distressed
    For a rainbow footing it nor he for his bónes rísen.

Gerard Manley Hopkins

Returning, We Hear the Larks

Sombre the night is,
And though we have our lives, we know
What sinister threat lurks there.

Dragging these anguished limbs, we only know
This poison-blasted track opens on our camp –
On a little safe sleep.

But hark! joy – joy – strange joy.
Lo! heights of night ringing with unseen larks.
Music showering our upturned list'ning faces.

Death could drop from the dark
As easily as song –
But song only dropped,
Like a blind man's dreams on the sand
By dangerous tides,
Like a girl's dark hair for she dreams no ruin lies there,
Or her kisses where a serpent hides.

Isaac Rosenberg

Skylarks

I

The lark begins to go up
Like a warning
As if the globe were uneasy –

Barrel-chested for heights,
Like an Indian of the high Andes,

A whippet head, barbed like a hunting arrow,

But leaden
With muscle
For the struggle
Against
Earth's centre.

And leaden
For ballast
In the rocketing storms of the breath.

Leaden
Like a bullet
To supplant
Life from its centre.

II

Crueller than owl or eagle

A towered bird, shot through the crested head
With the command, Not die

But climb

Climb

Sing

Obedient as to death a dead thing.

III

I suppose you just gape and let your gaspings
Rip in and out through your voicebox
                                        O lark

And sing inwards as well as outwards
Like a breaker of ocean milling the shingle
                                        O lark

O song, incomprehensibly both ways –
Joy! Help! Joy! Help!
                    O lark

IV

You stop to rest, far up, you teeter
Over the drop

But not stopping singing

Resting only for a second

Dropping just a little

Then up and up and up

Like a mouse with drowning fur
Bobbing and bobbing at the well-wall

Lamenting, mounting a little –

But the sun will not take notice
And the earth's centre smiles.

V

My idleness curdles
Seeing the lark labour near its cloud
Scrambling
In a nightmare difficulty
Up through the nothing

Its feathers thrash, its heart must be drumming like a motor,
As if it were too late, too late

Dithering in ether
Its song whirls faster and faster
And the sun whirls
The lark is evaporating
Till my eye's gossamer snaps
                    and my hearing floats back widely to earth

After which the sky lies blank open
Without wings, and the earth is a folded clod.

Only the sun goes silently and endlessly on with the lark's song.

All the dreary Sunday morning
Heaven is a madhouse
With the voices and frenzies of the larks,

Squealing and gibbering and cursing

Heads flung back, as I see them,
Wings almost torn off backwards – far up

Like sacrifices set floating
The cruel earth's offerings

The mad earth's missionaries.

VII

Like those flailing flames
That lift from the fling of a bonfire
Claws dangling full of what they feed on

The larks carry their tongues to the last atom
Battering and battering their last sparks out at the limit –
So it's a relief, a cool breeze
When they've had enough, when they're burned out
And the sun's sucked them empty
And the earth gives them the O.K.

And they relax, drifting with changed notes

Dip and float, not quite sure if they may
Then they are sure and they stoop

And maybe the whole agony was for this

The plummeting dead drop

With long cutting screams buckling like razors

But just before they plunge into the earth

They flare and glide off low over grass, then up
To land on a wall-top, crest up,
Weightless,
Paid-up,
Alert,

Conscience perfect.

VIII

Manacled with blood,
Cuchulain listened bowed,
Strapped to his pillar (not to die prone)
Hearing the far crow
Guiding the near lark nearer
With its blind song

'That some sorry little wight more feeble and misguided than thyself
Take thy head
Thine ear
And thy life's career from thee.'

Ted Hughes

The Skylark

The rolls and harrows lie at rest beside
The battered road and spreading far and wide
Above the russet clods the corn is seen
Sprouting its spiry points of tender green
Where squats the hare to terrors wide awake
Like some brown clod the harrows failed to break
While neath the warm hedge boys stray far from home
To crop the early blossoms as they come

Where buttercups will make them eager run
Opening their golden caskets to the sun
To see who shall be first to pluck the prize
And from their hurry up the skylark flies
And oer her half formed nest with happy wings
Winnows the air – till in the cloud she sings
Then hangs a dust spot in the sunny skies
And drops and drops till in her nest she lies
Where boys unheeding past – neer dreaming then
That birds which flew so high would drop again
To nests upon the ground where anything
May come at to destroy had they the wing
Like such a bird, themselves would be too proud
And build on nothing but a passing cloud
As free from danger as the heavens are free
From pain and toil – there would they build and be
And sail about the world to scenes unheard
Of and unseen – O were they but a bird
So think they while they listen to its song
And smile and fancy and so pass along
While its low nest moist with the dews of morn
Lies safely with the leveret in the corn

John Clare

Shelley's Skylark

(The Neighbourhood of Leghorn: March 1887)

Somewhere afield here something lies
In Earth's oblivious eyeless trust
That moved a poet to prophecies –
A pinch of unseen, unguarded dust:

The dust of the lark that Shelley heard,
And made immortal through times to be –
Though it only lived like another bird,
And knew not its immortality:

Lived its meek life; then, one day, fell –
A little ball of feather and bone;
And how it perished, when piped farewell,
And where it wastes, are alike unknown.

Maybe it rests in the loam I view,
Maybe it throbs in a myrtle's green,
Maybe it sleeps in the coming hue
Of a grape on the slopes of yon inland scene.

Go find it, faeries, go and find
That tiny pinch of priceless dust,
And bring a casket silver-lined,
And framed of gold that gems encrust;

And we will lay it safe therein,
And consecrate it to endless time;
For it inspired a bard to win
Ecstatic heights in thought and rhyme.

Thomas Hardy

Woodlark

The Woodlark

Teevo cheevo cheevio chee:
O where, what can thát be?
Weedio-weedio: there again!
So tiny a trickle of sóng-strain;

And all round not to be found
For brier, bough, furrow, or gréen ground
Before or behind or far or at hand
Either left either right
Anywhere in the súnlight.

Well, after all! Ah but hark –
'I am the little wóodlark.
The skylark is my cousin and he
Is known to men more than me.
Round a ring, around a ring
And while I sail (must listen) I sing.

To-day the sky is two and two
With white strokes and strains of the blue.
The blue wheat-acre is underneath
And the corn is corded and shoulders its sheaf,
The ear in milk, lush the sash,
And crush-silk poppies aflash,
The blood-gush blade-gash
Flame-rash rudred

Bud shelling or broad-shed
Tatter-tangled and dingle-a-danglèd
Dandy-hung dainty head.

And down . . . the furrow dry
Sunspurge and oxeye
And lace-leaved lovely
Foam-tuft fumitory.

I ám so véry, O só very glád
That I dó thínk there is not to be had
[Anywhere any more joy to be in.
Cheevio:] when the cry within
Says Go on then I go on
Till the longing is less and the good gone,
But down drop, if it says Stop,
To the all-a-leaf of the tréetop.
And after that off the bough
[Hover-float to the hedge brow.]

Through the velvety wind V-winged
[Where shake shadow is sun's-eye-ringed]
To the nest's nook I balance and buoy
With a sweet joy of a sweet joy,
Sweet, of a sweet, of a sweet joy
Of a sweet – a sweet – sweet – joy.'

                                Gerard Manley Hopkins

Swallow

Anacreon's Ode to the Swallow

Thou indeed, little Swallow
A sweet yearly comer,
Art building a hollow
New nest every summer,
And straight dost depart
Where no gazing can follow,
Past Memphis, down Nile!
Ah! but Love all the while
Builds his nest in my heart,
Through the cold winter weeks:
And as one Love takes flight,
Comes another, O Swallow,
In an egg warm and white,
And another is callow.
And the large gaping beaks
Chirp all day and all night:
And the Loves who are older
Help the young and the poor Loves,
And the young Loves grow bolder
Increase by the score Loves –
Why, what can be done?
If a noise comes from one,
Can I bear all this rout of a hundred and more Loves?

Elizabeth Barrett Browning

Itylus

Swallow, my sister, O sister swallow,
  How can thine heart be full of the spring?
    A thousand summers are over and dead.
What hast thou found in the spring to follow?
  What hast thou found in thine heart to sing?
    What wilt thou do when the summer is shed?

O swallow, sister, O fair swift swallow,
  Why wilt thou fly after spring to the south,
    The soft south whither thine heart is set?
Shall not the grief of the old time follow?
  Shall not the song thereof cleave to thy mouth?
    Hast thou forgotten ere I forget?

Sister, my sister, O fleet sweet swallow,
  Thy way is long to the sun and the south;
    But I, fulfilled of my heart's desire,
Shedding my song upon height, upon hollow,
  From tawny body and sweet small mouth
    Feed the heart of the night with fire.

I the nightingale all spring through,
  O swallow, sister, O changing swallow,
    All spring through till the spring be done,
Clothed with the light of the night on the dew,
  Sing, while the hours and the wild birds follow,
    Take flight and follow and find the sun.

Sister, my sister, O soft light swallow,
   Though all things feast in the spring's
        guest-chamber,
      How hast thou heart to be glad thereof yet?
For where thou fliest I shall not follow,
   Till life forget and death remember,
      Till thou remember and I forget.

Swallow, my sister, O singing swallow,
   I know not how thou hast heart to sing.
      Hast thou the heart? is it all past over?
Thy lord the summer is good to follow,
   And fair the feet of thy lover the spring:
      But what wilt thou say to the spring thy lover?

O swallow, sister, O fleeting swallow,
   My heart in me is a molten ember
      And over my head the waves have met.
But thou wouldst tarry or I would follow,
   Could I forget or thou remember,
      Couldst thou remember and I forget.

O sweet stray sister, O shifting swallow,
   The heart's division divideth us.
      Thy heart is light as a leaf of a tree;
But mine goes forth among sea-gulfs hollow
   To the place of the slaying of Itylus,
      The feast of Daulis, the Thracian sea.

O swallow, sister, O rapid swallow,
   I pray thee sing not a little space.
      Are not the roofs and the lintels wet?
The woven web that was plain to follow,
   The small slain body, the flowerlike face,
      Can I remember if thou forget?

O sister, sister, thy first-begotten!
　　The hands that cling and the feet that follow,
　　The voice of the child's blood crying yet
Who hath remembered me? who hath forgotten?
　　Thou hast forgotten, O summer swallow,
　　　But the world shall end when I forget.

Algernon Charles Swinburne

A Swallow

Has slipped through a fracture in the snow-sheet
Which is still our sky –

She flicks past, ahead of her name,
Twinkling away out over the lake.

Reaching this way and that way, with her scissors,
Snipping midges
Trout are still too numb and sunken to stir for.

Sahara clay ovens, at mirage heat,
Glazed her blues, and still she is hot.

She wearied of snatching clegs off the lugs of buffaloes
And of lassooing the flirt-flags of gazelles.

They told her the North was one giant snowball
Rolling South. She did not believe them.
So she exchanged the starry chart of Columbus
For a beggar's bowl of mud.

Setting her compass-tremor tail-needles
She harpooned a wind
That wallowed in the ocean,
Working her barbs deeper
Through that twisting mass she came –

Did she close her eyes and trust in God?
No, she saw lighthouses
Streaming in chaos
Like sparks from a chimney –
She had fixed her instruments on home.

And now, suddenly, into a blanch-tree stillness
A silence of celandines,
A fringing and stupor of frost
She bursts, weightless –
                              to anchor
On eggs frail as frost.

There she goes, flung taut on her leash,
Her eyes at her mouth-corners,
Water-skiing out across a wind
That wrecks great flakes against windscreens.

Ted Hughes

Augury

Magnetic winds from the sun pour in
and send our instruments akimbo.
Nothing runs like clockwork now.
As skeletal clouds unwreathe our exposure,
panicky citizens climb ladders to hammer
their roofs on harder. A crackle of static,

and the world's fat face is in shadow.
There are swallow nests under the eaves,
each with a staring cargo: six bronze bibs,
six black-masked, African birds. They dip
and snap the last bees up. A million Ms
foregather with a million others on the sky.
This is the shape that memory takes.
For days they practise flying, then they fly.

                              Caitríona O'Reilly

Swallows

I wish my whole battened
heart were a property
like this, with swallows
in every room – so at ease

they twitter and preen
from the picture frames
like an audience in the gods
before an opera

and in the mornings
wheel above my bed
in a mockery of pity
before winging it

up the stairwell
to stream out into light

                              Kathleen Jamie

The Swallows' Nest

(for P. B.)

Shutters, broken,
firewood, a rake, a wrought–
iron bed, the torch–lit
rafters of the lumber-room,
you showing me

one bird tucked in a home–
made bracket of spittle
and earth, while its mate slept
perched on the rim, at an angle
exact as a raised latch.

Kathleen Jamie

The Swallow

Foolish prater, what dost thou
So early at my window do
With thy tuneless serenade?
Well't had been had Tereus made
Thee as dumb as Philomel;
There his knife had done but well.
In thy undiscovered nest,
Thou dost all the winter rest,
And dreamest o'er thy summer joys,
Free from the stormy season's noise,
Free from th'ill thou'st done to me:
Who disturbs, or seeks out thee?
Hadst thou all the charming notes

Of the wood's poetic throats,
All thy art could never pay
What thou'st ta'en from me away.
Cruel bird, thou'st ta'en away
A dream out of my arms today,
A dream that ne'er must equalled be
By all that waking eyes may see.
Thou this damage to repair,
Nothing half so sweet or fair,
Nothing half so good canst bring,
Though men say thou bringst the spring.

Abraham Cowley

Tree Swallow

Feathering

Yesterday she took down from the attic
an old lumpy tea-colored pillow – stained
with drool, hair grease, night sweats, or what!
which many heads may have waked upon
in the dark, and lain there motionless, eyes open,
wondering at the strangeness within themselves –
took it and ripped out the stitching
at one end, making of it a sack.

Standing on a bench in the garden,
she plunges a hand into the sack and lifts
out a puffy fistful of feathers.
A few accidentally spill and drift,
and tree swallows appear. She raises
the hand holding the feathers straight up
over her head, and stands like a god
of seedtime about to scatter bits of plenitude,
or like herself in a long-ago summer, by a pond,
chumming for sunfish with bread crumbs.

When the breeze quickens she opens
her fist and more of these fluffs
near zero on the scale of materiality
float free. One of the swallows
now looping and whirling about her
snatches at a feather, misses, twists round

on itself, streaks back, snaps its beak
shut on it, and flings itself across the field.
Another swallow seizes a feather
and flies up, but, flapping and turning,
loses it to a third swallow, who soars
with it even higher and disappears.

After many tosses, misses, parries, catches,
she ties off the pillow, ending for now
the game they make of it when she's there,
the imperative to feather one's nest,
which has come down in the tree swallow
from the Pliocene. She returns to the house,
a slight lurch in her gait – not surprising,
for she has been so long at play with these
acrobatic, daredevil aerialists, she might
momentarily have lost the trick of walking on earth.

Galway Kinnell

Wagtail

Wagtail and Baby

A baby watched a ford, whereto
  A wagtail came for drinking;
A blaring bull went wading through,
  The wagtail showed no shrinking.

A stallion splashed his way across,
  The birdie nearly sinking;
He gave his plumes a twitch and toss,
  And held his own unblinking.

Next saw the baby round the spot
  A mongrel slowly slinking;
The wagtail gazed, but faltered not
  In dip and sip and prinking.

A perfect gentleman then neared;
  The wagtail, in a winking,
With terror rose and disappeared;
  The baby fell a-thinking.

Thomas Hardy

Dipper

The Dipper

It was winter, near freezing,
I'd walked through a forest of firs
when I saw issue out of the waterfall
a solitary bird.

It lit on a damp rock,
and, as water swept stupidly on,
wrung from its own throat
supple, undammable song.

It isn't mine to give.
I can't coax this bird to my hand
that knows the depth of the river
yet sings of it on land.

Kathleen Jamie

Wren

The Cock's Nest

The spring my father died – it was winter, really,
February fill-grave, but March was in
By the time we felt the bruise of it and knew
How empty the rooms were – that spring
A wren flew to our yard, over Walter Willson's
Warehouse roof and the girls' school playground
From the old allotments that are now no more than a compost
For raising dockens and cats. It found a niche
Tucked behind the pipe of the bathroom outflow,
Caged in a wickerwork of creeper; then
Began to build:
Three times a minute, hour after hour,
Backward and forward to the backyard wall,
Nipping off neb-fulls of the soot-spored moss
Rooted between the bricks. In a few days
The nest was finished. They say the cock
Leases an option of sites and leaves the hen
To choose which nest she will. She didn't choose our yard.
And as March gambolled out, the fat King-Alfred sun
Blared down too early from its tinny trumpet
On new-dug potato-beds, the still bare creeper,
The cock's nest with never an egg in,
And my father dead.

Norman Nicholson

Wren

Who owns
Each tail-feather barred like a falcon?
He does – that freckled inspector

Of the woodland's vaults. Burglar
Alarm of the undergrowth. King
Of the lowest hovel of winter bramble.

The wren is a nervous wreck
Since he saw the sun from the back of an eagle.
He prefers to creep. If he can't creep

He'll whirr trickle-low as his shadow –
Brief as a mouse's bounce from safety to safety.
Even the ermine snow-flake's nose can't start him –

When the thicket's drifted, a shrouded corpse,
He's in under there, ticking,
Not as a last pulse, but a new life waiting.

Lonely keeper of the gold
In the tumbled cleave.
A bird out of Merlin's ear.

Silent watcher. Suddenly
Singing, like a martyr on fire,
Glossolalia.

Ted Hughes

Taxonomy

Wren. Full song. No subsong. Call of alarm, spreketh & ought
damage the eyes with its form, small body, tail pricked up &
    beak like a hair

trailed through briars & at a distance scored with lime scent in
    the nose
like scrapings from a goldsmith's cuttle, rock alum & fair butter
    well-temped

which script goes is unrecognised by this one, is pulled by the ear
in anger the line at fault is under and inwardly drear as a bridge
    in winter

reared up inotherwise to seal the eyes through darkness, the
    bridge speaks
it does not speak, the starlings speak that steal the speech of men,
    uc antea

a spark that meets the idea of itself, apparently fearless.
Ah cruelty. And I had not stopped to think upon it

& I had not extended it into the world for love for naught.

Helen Macdonald

Northern Mockingbird

Bird-Witted

With innocent wide penguin eyes, three
    large fledgling mocking-birds below
the pussy-willow tree,
    stand in a row,
wings touching, feebly solemn,
till they see
        their no longer larger
        mother bringing
something which will partially
feed one of them.

Toward the high-keyed intermittent squeak
    of broken carriage-springs, made by
the three similar, meek-
    coated bird's-eye
freckled forms she comes; and when
from the beak
        of one, the still living
        beetle has dropped
out, she picks it up and puts
it in again.

Standing in the shade till they have dressed
    their thickly filamented, pale
pussy-willow-surfaced
    coats, they spread tail

and wings, showing one by one,
the modest
    white stripe lengthwise on the
    tail and crosswise
underneath the wing, and the
accordion

is closed again. What delightful note
   with rapid unexpected flute-
sounds leaping from the throat
   of the astute
grown bird comes back to one from
the remote
    unenergetic sun-
    lit air before
the brood was here? How harsh
the bird's voice has become.

A piebald cat observing them,
   is slowly creeping toward the trim
trio on the tree-stem.
   Unused to him
the three make room – uneasy
new problem.
    A dangling foot that missed
    its grasp is raised
and finds the twig on which it
planned to perch. The

parent darting down, nerved by what chills
   the blood, and by hope rewarded –
of toil – since nothing fills
   squeaking unfed
mouths, wages deadly combat,
and half kills
    with bayonet beak and

cruel wings, the
intellectual cautious-
ly c r e e p ing cat.

Marianne Moore

Patch Work

The bird book says, common, conspicuous.
This time of year all day
The mockingbird
Sweeps at a moderate height
Above the densely flowering
Suburban plots of May,
The characteristic shine
Of white patch cutting through the curved ash-grey
That bars each wing;
Or it appears to us
Perched on the post that ends a washing-line
To sing there, as in flight,
A repertoire of songs that it has heard
– From other birds, and others of its kind –
Which it has recombined
And made its own, especially one
With a few separate plangent notes begun
Then linking trills as a long confident run
Toward the immediate distance,
Repeated all day through
In the sexual longings of the spring
(Which also are derivative)
And almost mounting to
Fulfilment, thus to give
Such muscular vigour to a note so strong,
Fulfilment that does not destroy

The original, still–unspent
Longings that led it where it went
But links them in a bird's inhuman joy
Lifted upon the wing
Of that patched body, that insistence
Which fills the gardens up with headlong song.

Thom Gunn

Song

The Sub-Song

For Richard Mabey

I thought it a piece of fancifulness
when first I heard it mentioned:

the sub-song of the wintering bird:

but no, it's a scientific
classification of sound, denoting

a drowsily territorial
foreshadow, rehearsal or update,

sung past the leafless tree
in a minor key.

With no particular
dedicatee.

Or recitative between arias,
summer and summer,

song of the slumbering, fixate
middle-comer.

I think I have caught the sub-song sounded
in various winter bars

by singletons with their beaks buried under

their shoulders, or in supermarkets,
wobbling alone a trolley,

with one wheel
out of true:

far from the buzzard's mew
or the squawk of hawk on wrist,

crying, I fly, I can sing, I am here, I exist,
perpetually,

but it might have been nothing, or there again,
might have been me.

Kit Wright

Everyone Sang

Everyone suddenly burst out singing;
And I was filled with such delight
As prisoned birds must find in freedom,
Winging wildly across the white
Orchards and dark green fields; on; on; and out of sight.

Everyone's voice was suddenly lifted;
And beauty came like the setting sun:
My heart was shaken with tears; and horror

Drifted away . . . O, but Everyone
Was a bird; and the song was wordless; the singing will never
    be done.

The Language of Birds

Do you ask what the birds say? The Sparrow, the Dove,
The Linnet and Thrush say, 'I love and I love!'
In the winter they're silent – the wind is so strong;
What it says, I don't know, but it sings a loud song.
But green leaves, and blossoms, and sunny warm weather,
And singing, and loving – all come back together.
But the Lark is so brimful of gladness and love,
The green fields below him, the blue sky above,
That he sings, and he sings; and for ever sings he –
'I love my Love, and my Love loves me!'

Samuel Taylor Coleridge

Ornithological Petrarchan

It is difficult to portray bird voices in writing, because birds
rarely make 'human' sounds, and our interpretations vary: one
person hears a call-note as 'teu', another as 'chew' or 'sioo'.
            Peterson, Mountfort & Hollom,
    A Field Guide to the Birds of Britain and Europe (Collins)

    Calidris maritima pipes '*weak wit*',
    Gypaetus barbatus thinly cries '*queer*',
    the Pheasant's '*cork cock*' oft' delights the ear,

the Little Stint, when flushed, has a sharp *'tit'*,
Calidris alba calls on us to *'quit'*,
the Reed Bunting's alarm call *'shit'* rings clear.
Is this *Calidris canutus* we hear?
Hark! a low *'nut'*, in flight, a whistling *'twit'*.

But what is this deep sighing *'oo-oo-oo'*
more moaning than *Strix aluco*? *'Quick quick!'*
Turnix sylvatica's *'croo croo crooo CROOO'*
bursts from a bush. A hard explosive *'prik'*
(from *Coccothraustes coccothraustes*) sends
exciting vibes to sensitive nerve-ends.

Peter Reading

Serenades

The Irish nightingale
Is a sedge-warbler,
A little bird with a big voice
Kicking up a racket all night.

Not what you'd expect
From the musical nation.
I haven't even heard one –
Nor an owl, for that matter.

My serenades have been
The broken voice of a crow
In a draught or a dream,
The wheeze of bats

Or the ack-ack
Of the tramp corncrake
Lost in a no man's land
Between combines and chemicals.

So fill the bottles, love,
Leave them inside their cots.
And if they do wake us, well,
So would the sedge-warbler.

Seamus Heaney

On a Bird Singing in its Sleep

A bird half wakened in the lunar noon
Sang halfway through its little inborn tune.
Partly because it sang but once all night
And that from no especial bush's height,
Partly because it sang ventriloquist
And had the inspiration to desist
Almost before the prick of hostile ears,
It ventured less in peril than appears.
It could not have come down to us so far,
Through the interstices of things ajar
On the long bead chain of repeated birth,
To be a bird while we are men on earth,
If singing out of sleep and dream that way
Had made it much more easily a prey.

Robert Frost

The Spring Call

Down Wessex way, when spring's a-shine,
  The blackbird's 'pret-ty de-urr!'
In Wessex accents marked as mine
  Is heard afar and near.

He flutes it strong, as if in song
  No R's of feebler tone
Than his appear in 'pretty dear,'
  Have blackbirds ever known.

Yet they pipe 'prattie deerh!' I glean,
  Beneath a Scottish sky,
And 'pehty de-aw!' amid the treen
  Of Middlesex or nigh.

While some folk say – perhaps in play –
  Who know the Irish isle,
'Tis 'purrity dare!' in treeland there
  When songsters would beguile.

Well: I'll say what the listening birds
  Say, hearing 'pret-ty de-urr!' –
However strangers sound such words,
  That's how we sound them here.

Yes, in this clime at pairing time,
  As soon as eyes can see her
At dawn of day, the proper way
  To call is 'pret-ty de-urr!'

Thomas Hardy

Birds All Singing

Something to do with territory makes them sing,
Or so we are told – they woo no sweet and fair,
But tantalise and transfigure the morning air
With coarse descriptions of any other cock bird
That dare intrude a wing
In their half-acre – bumptious and absurd.

Come out and fight, they cry, and roulades of
Tumbling-down sweetness and ascending bliss
Elaborate unrepeatable ancestries;
And impossible deformities still to come
Rise like angels above
The tenement windows of their sylvan slum.

Not passion but possession. A miserly
Self-enlargement that muddles mine and me
Says the half-acre is the bird, and he,
Deluded to that grandeur, swells, and with
A jolly roundelay
Of boasts and curses establishes a myth.

The human figure underneath the boughs
Takes strictly down, as false as a machine,
The elements of the seen or the half-seen,
And with the miracle of his ear notes all
The singing bird allows,
And feels it innocent, calls it pastoral.

Creations clumsily collide and make
The bird and man more separate. The man,
Caught up in the lie the bird began,
Feigns a false acre that the world can't hold
Where all is for his sake;
It is the touchstone proving him true gold.

So he, his own enlargement also, thinks
A quiet thought in his corner that creates
Territories of existence, private states
Of being where trespassers are shot at sight;
And myth within myth blinks
Its blind eyes on the casual morning light.

Under or over, nothing truly lies
In its own lucidity. Creation moves
Restlessly through all its hates or loves
And leaves a wild scenario in its place
Where birds shake savage cries
Like clenched fists in the world's uncaring face.

And man, with straws of singing in his hair,
Strolls in his Bedlam transfiguring every fact,
In full possession of what he never lacked,
The power of being not himself – till with
A twitch of the morning air
Time topples bird and man out of their myth.

                                        Norman MacCaig

She Dotes

She dotes on what the wild birds say
Or hint or mock at, night and day, —
Thrush, blackbird, all that sing in May,
　　And songless plover,
Hawk, heron, owl, and woodpecker.
They never say a word to her
　　About her lover.
She laughs at them for childishness,
She cries at them for carelessness
Who see her going loverless
　　Yet sing and chatter
Just as when he was not a ghost,
Nor ever ask her what she has lost
　　Or what is the matter.
Yet she has fancied blackbirds hide
A secret, and that thrushes chide
Because she thinks death can divide
　　Her from her lover;
And she has slept, trying to translate
The word the cuckoo cries to his mate
　　Over and over.

Edward Thomas

Robin

from The White Devil

Call for the Robin-Red-brest and the wren,
Since ore shadie groves they hover,
And with leaves and flowres doe cover
The friendlesse bodies of unburied men.
Call unto his funerall Dole
The Ante, the field-mouse, and the mole
To reare him hillockes, that shall keepe him warme,
And (when gay tombes are rob'd) sustaine no harme,
But keepe the wolfe far thence, that's foe to men,
For with his nailes hee'l dig them up agen.

John Webster

Nightingale

Sonnet

O nightingale, that on yon bloomy spray
   Warbl'st at eve, when all the woods are still,
   Thou with fresh hope the lover's heart dost fill,
   While the jolly hours lead on propitious May;
Thy liquid notes that close the eye of day,
   First heard before the shallow cuckoo's bill,
   Portend success in love: O if Jove's will
   Have linkt that amorous power to thy soft lay,
Now timely sing, ere the rude bird of hate
   Foretell my hopeless doom in some grove nigh,
   As thou from year to year hast sung too late
For my relief, yet hadst no reason why:
   Whether the muse or love call thee his mate,
   Both them I serve, and of their train am I.

John Milton

To the Nightingale

Which the author heard sing on New-Year's Day, 1792

Whence is it, that amaz'd I hear
   From yonder wither'd spray,
This foremost morn of all the year,
   The melody of May?

And why, since thousands would be proud
   Of such a favour shewn,
Am I selected from the crowd,
   To witness it alone?

Sing'st thou, sweet Philomel, to me,
   For that I also long
Have practis'd in the groves like thee,
   Though not like thee in song?

Or sing'st thou rather under force
   Of some divine command,
Commission'd to presage a course
   Of happier days at hand?

Thrice welcome then! for many a long
   And joyless year have I,
As thou to-day, put forth my song
   Beneath a wintry sky.

But thee no wintry skies can harm,
   Who only need'st to sing,
To make ev'n January charm,
   And ev'ry season Spring.

William Cowper

Ode to a Nightingale

My heart aches, and a drowsy numbness pains
  My sense, as though of hemlock I had drunk,
Or emptied some dull opiate to the drains
  One minute past, and Lethe-wards had sunk:
'Tis not through envy of thy happy lot,
  But being too happy in thine happiness –
    That thou, light-wingèd Dryad of the trees,
      In some melodious plot
  Of beechen green, and shadows numberless,
    Singest of summer in full-throated ease.

O, for a draught of vintage! that hath been
  Cooled a long age in the deep-delvèd earth,
Tasting of Flora and the country green,
  Dance, and Provençal song, and sunburnt mirth!
O for a beaker full of the warm South,
  Full of the true, the blushful Hippocrene,
    With beaded bubbles winking at the brim,
      And purple-stainèd mouth,
  That I might drink, and leave the world unseen,
    And with thee fade away into the forest dim –

Fade far away, dissolve, and quite forget
  What thou among the leaves hast never known,
The weariness, the fever, and the fret
  Here, where men sit and hear each other groan;
Where palsy shakes a few, sad, last grey hairs,
  Where youth grows pale, and spectre-thin, and dies;
    Where but to think is to be full of sorrow
      And leaden-eyed despairs;
  Where Beauty cannot keep her lustrous eyes,
    Or new Love pine at them beyond to-morrow.

Away! away! for I will fly to thee,
  Not charioted by Bacchus and his pards,
But on the viewless wings of Poesy,
  Though the dull brain perplexes and retards.
Already with thee! tender is the night,
  And haply the Queen-Moon is on her throne,
    Clustered around by all her starry Fays;
      But here there is no light,
  Save what from heaven is with the breezes blown
    Through verdurous glooms and winding mossy
      ways.

I cannot see what flowers are at my feet,
  Nor what soft incense hangs upon the boughs,
But, in embalmèd darkness, guess each sweet
  Wherewith the seasonable month endows
The grass, the thicket, and the fruit-tree wild –
  White hawthorn, and the pastoral eglantine;
    Fast fading violets covered up in leaves;
      And mid-May's eldest child,
  The coming musk-rose, full of dewy wine,
    The murmurous haunt of flies on summer eves.

Darkling I listen; and, for many a time
  I have been half in love with easeful Death,
Called him soft names in many a musèd rhyme,
  To take into the air my quiet breath;
Now more than ever seems it rich to die,
  To cease upon the midnight with no pain,
    While thou art pouring forth thy soul abroad
      In such an ecstasy!
  Still wouldst thou sing, and I have ears in vain –
    To thy high requiem become a sod.

Thou wast not born for death, immortal Bird!
 No hungry generations tread thee down;
The voice I hear this passing night was heard
 In ancient days by emperor and clown:
Perhaps the self-same song that found a path
 Through the sad heart of Ruth, when, sick for home,
  She stood in tears amid the alien corn;
   The same that oft-times hath
 Charmed magic casements, opening on the foam
 Of perilous seas, in faery lands forlorn.

Forlorn! the very word is like a bell
 To toll me back from thee to my sole self!
Adieu! the fancy cannot cheat so well
 As she is famed to do, deceiving elf.
Adieu! adieu! thy plaintive anthem fades
 Past the near meadows, over the still stream,
  Up the hill-side; and now 'tis buried deep
   In the next valley-glades:
 Was it a vision, or a waking dream?
 Fled is that music – Do I wake or sleep?

John Keats

Early Nightingale

When first we hear the shy come nightingales
They seem to mutter o er their songs in fear
And climb we eer so soft the spinney rails
All stops as if no bird was anywhere
The kindled bushes with the young leaves thin
Let curious eyes to search a long way in
Until impatience cannot see or hear
The hidden music gets but little way

Upon the path when up the songs begin
Full loud a moment and then low again
But when a day or two confirms her stay
Boldly she sings and loud for half the day
And soon the village brings the woodmans tale
Of having heard the new-come nightingale

John Clare

The Nightingale's Nest

Up this green woodland ride lets softly rove
And list the nightingale – she dwelleth here
Hush! let the woodgate softly clap – for fear
The noise might drive her from her home of love
For here Ive heard her many a merry year
At morn, at eve nay all the live long day
As though she lived on song – this very spot
Just where that old mans beard all wildly trails
Rude arbours o er the road and stops the way
And where that child its blue bell flowers hath got
Laughing and creeping through the mossy rails
There have I hunted like a very boy
Creeping on hands and knees through matted thorn
To find her nest and see her feed her young
And vainly did I many hours employ
All seemed as hidden as a thought unborn
And where those crimping fern leaves ramp among
The hazels under boughs – Ive nestled down
And watched her while she sung – and her renown
Hath made me marvel that so famed a bird
Should have no better dress than russet brown
Her wings would tremble in her exstacy
And feathers stand on end as twere with joy

And mouth wide open to release her heart
Of its out sobbing songs – the happiest part
Of summers fame she shared – for so to me
Did happy fancys shapen her employ
But if I touched a bush or scarcely stirred
All in a moment stopt – I watched in vain
The timid bird had left the hazel bush
And at a distance hid to sing again
Lost in a wilderness of listening leaves
Rich exstacy would pour its luscious strain
Till envy spurred the emulating thrush
To start less wild and scarce inferior songs
For cares with him for half the year remain
To damp the ardour of his speckled breast
The nightingale to summers life belongs
And naked trees and winters nipping wrongs
Are strangers to her music and her rest
Her joys are evergreen her world is wide
– Hark there she is as usual let's be hush
For in this black thorn clump if rightly guessed
Her curious house is hidden – part aside
These hazel branches in a gentle way
And stoop right cautious neath the rustling boughs
For we will have another search today
And hunt this fern strown thorn clump round and round
And where this seeded wood grass idly bows
Well wade right through – it is a likely nook
In such like spots and often on the ground
Theyll build where rude boys never think to look
Aye as I live – her secret nest is here
Upon this whitethorn stulp – I've searched about
For hours in vain – there put that bramble bye
Nay trample on its branches and get near.
How subtle is the bird she started out
And raised a plaintive note of danger nigh
Ere we were past the brambles and now near

Her nest she sudden stops – as chaking fear
That might betray her home so even now
Well leave it as we found it – safetys guard
Of pathless solitudes shall keep it still
See there shes sitting on the old oak bough
Mute in her fears our presence doth retard
Her joys and doubt turns every rapture chill
Sing on sweet bird may no worse hap befall
Thy visions then the fear that now decieves.
We will not plunder music of its dower
Nor turn this spot of happiness to thrall
For melody seems hid in every flower
That blossoms near thy home – these harebells all
Seems bowing with the beautiful in song
And gaping cuckoo with its spotted leaves
Seems blushing with the singing it has heard
How curious is the nest no other bird
Uses such loose materials or weaves
Its dwelling in such spots – dead oaken leaves
Are placed without and velvet moss within
And little scraps of grass – and scant and spare
What scarcely seem materials down and hair
For from mans haunts she nothing seems to win
Yet nature is the builder and contrives
Homes for her childrens comfort even here
Where solitudes disciples spend their lives
Unseen save when a wanderer passes near
That loves such pleasant places – deep adown
The nest is made an hermits mossy cell.
Snug lie her curious eggs in number five
Of deadened green or rather olive brown
And the old prickly thorn bush guards them well
So here well leave them still unknown to wrong
As the old woodlands legacy of song

John Clare

The Nightingales

Three I heard once together in Barrow Hill Copse –
At midnight, with a slip of moon, in a sort of dusk.
They were not shy, heard us, and continued uttering their notes.

But after 'Adelaide' and the poets / ages of/ praise
How could I think such beautiful; or ~~gather the lies~~ / utter false
    the lies/
Fit for verse, it was only bird–song, a midnight strange new
    noise.

But a month before a laughing linnet /in the gold/ had sung
/(And green)/ As if poet or musician had never/ before/ true
    tongue
To tell out nature's magic with any truth ~~held~~ /kept for/
    long . . .

By Fretherne lane the linnet /(in the green)/ I shall not forget
/(Nor gold)/ The start of wonder – the joy to be so in debt
To beauty – to the hidden bird there in ~~elms /green/ great~~ /
    Spring elms elate./

Should I then lie, because at midnight one had nightingales,
Singing a mile off in the young oaks – that wake to look to
    Wales,
~~And~~ /Dream and/ watch Severn – like me, will tell no false /
    adoration in/ tales?

Ivor Gurney

'Herewith, a deep-delv'd draught'

Herewith, a deep-delv'd draught to *Luscinia*
    megarhynchos . . .

but it wasn't *jug-jug* I heard that night on the
    outskirts of Mostar,

night of torrential rain, before the
    bridge was bisected,

it was a cadence of ominous harmony
    not to be heard since,

and *was* forlorn, and the very sound seemed,
    yes, like a tolling.

Peter Reading

Redstart

The Firetail's Nest

Tweet pipes the robin as the cat creeps bye
Her nestling young that in the elderns lie
And then the bluecap tootles in its glee
Picking the flies from blossomed apple tree
And pink the chaffinch cries its well known strain
Urging its mate to utter pink again
While in a quiet mood hedgsparrows trie
An inward stir of shadowed melody
While on the rotten tree the firetail mourns
As the old hedger to his toil returns
And chops the grain to stop the gap close bye
The hole where her blue eggs in safety lie
Of every thing that stirs she dreameth wrong
And pipes her 'tweet tut' fears the whole day long

John Clare

Wheatear

The Wheat-Ear

From that deep shelter'd solitude,
Where in some quarry wild and rude,
Your feather'd mother reared her brood,
        Why, pilgrim, did you brave,
The upland winds so bleak and keen,
To seek these hills? whose slopes between
Wide stretch'd in grey expanse is seen,
        The Ocean's toiling wave?

Did instinct bid you linger here,
That broad and restless Ocean near,
And wait, till with the waning year
        Those northern gales arise,
Which, from the tall cliff's rugged side
Shall give your soft light plumes to glide,
Across the channel's refluent tide,
        To seek more favoring skies?

Alas! and has not instinct said
That luxury's toils for you are laid,
And that by groundless fears betray'd
        You ne'er perhaps may know
Those regions, where the embowering vine
Loves round the luscious fig to twine,
And mild the Suns of Winter shine,
        And flowers perennial blow.

To take you, shepherd boys prepare
The hollow turf, the wiry snare,
Of those weak terrors well aware,
        That bid you vainly dread
The shadows floating o'er the downs,
Or murmuring gale, that round the stones
Of some old beacon, as it moans,
        Scarce moves the thistle's head.

And if a cloud obscure the Sun
With faint and fluttering heart you run,
And to the pitfall you should shun
        Resort in trembling haste;
While, on that dewy cloud so high,
The lark, sweet minstrel of the sky,
Sings in the morning's beamy eye,
        And bathes his spotted breast.

Ah! simple bird, resembling you
Are those, that with distorted view
Thro' life some selfish end pursue,
        With low inglorious aim;
They sink in blank oblivious night,
While minds superior dare the light,
And high on honor's glorious height
        Aspire to endless fame.

                Charlotte Smith

Song Thrush

The Throstle

'Summer is coming, summer is coming.
　　I know it, I know it, I know it.
Light again, leaf again, life again, love again,'
　　Yes, my wild little poet.

Sing the new year in under the blue.
　　Last year you sang it as gladly.
'New, new, new, new!' Is it then *so* new
　　That you should carol so madly?

'Love again, song again, nest again, young again,'
　　Never a prophet so crazy!
And hardly a daisy as yet, little friend,
　　See, there is hardly a daisy.

'Here again, here, here, here, happy year!'
　　O warble unchidden, unbidden!
Summer is coming, is coming, my dear,
　　And all the winters are hidden.

Alfred, Lord Tennyson

Evening Thrush

Beyond a twilight of limes and willows
The church craftsman is still busy –
Switing idols,
Rough pre-Goidelic gods and goddesses,
Out of old bits of churchyard yew.

Suddenly flinging
Everything off, head-up, flame-naked,
Plunges shuddering into the creator –

Then comes plodding back, with a limp, over cobbles.

That was a virtuoso's joke.

Now, serious, stretched full height, he aims
At the zenith. He situates a note
Right on the source of light.

Sews a seamless garment, simultaneously
Hurls javelins of dew
Three in air together, catches them.

Explains a studied theorem of sober practicality.

Cool-eyed,
Gossips in a mundane code of splutters
With Venus and Jupiter.
                              Listens –
Motionless, intent astronomer.

Suddenly launches a soul –

The first roses hand in a yoke stupor.
Globe after globe rolls out
Through his fluteful of dew –

The tree-stacks ride out on the widening arc.

Alone and darkening
At the altar of a star
With his sword through his throat
The thrush of clay goes on arguing
Over the graves.

O thrush,
If that really is you, behind the leaf-screen,
Who is this –

Worn-headed, on the lawn's grass, after sunset,
Humped, voiceless, turdus, imprisoned
As a long-distance lorry-driver, dazed

With the pop and static and unending
Of worms and wife and kids?

Ted Hughes

Mistle Thrush

The Darkling Thrush

I leant upon a coppice gate
   When Frost was spectre-gray,
And Winter's dregs made desolate
   The weakening eye of day.
The tangled bine-stems scored the sky
   Like strings of broken lyres,
And all mankind that haunted nigh
   Had sought their household fires.

The land's sharp features seemed to be
   The Century's corpse outleant,
His crypt the cloudy canopy,
   The wind his death-lament.
The ancient pulse of germ and birth
   Was shrunken hard and dry,
And every spirit upon earth
   Seemed fervourless as I.

At once a voice arose among
   The bleak twigs overhead
In a full-hearted evensong
   Of joy illimited;
An aged thrush, frail, gaunt, and small,
   In blast-beruffled plume,
Had chosen thus to fling his soul
   Upon the growing gloom.

So little cause for carolings
  Of such ecstatic sound
Was written on terrestrial things
  Afar or nigh around,
That I could think there trembled through
  His happy good-night air
Some blessed Hope, whereof he knew
  And I was unaware.

Thomas Hardy

The Thrush

When Winter's ahead,
What can you read in November
That you read in April
When Winter's dead?

I hear the thrush, and I see
Him alone at the end of the lane
Near the bare poplar's tip,
Singing continuously.

Is it more that you know
Than that, even as in April,
So in November,
Winter is gone that must go?

Or is all your lore
Not to call November November,
And April April,
And Winter Winter – no more?

But I know the months all,
And their sweet names, April,
May and June and October,
As you call and call

I must remember
What died into April
And consider what will be born
Of a fair November;

And April I love for what
It was born of, and November
For what it will die in,
What they are and what they are not,

While you love what is kind,
What you can sing in
And love and forget in
All that's ahead and behind.

Edward Thomas

Thrush

The Thrush

Music of a thrush, clearbright
Lovable language of light,
Heard I under a birchtree
Yesterday, all grace and glee –
Was ever so sweet a thing
Fine-plaited as his whistling?

Matins, he reads the lesson,
A chasuble of plumage on.
His cry from a grove, his brightshout
Over countrysides rings out,
Hill prophet, maker of moods,
Passion's bright bard of glenwoods.
Every voice of the brookside
Sings he, in his darling pride,
Every sweet-metred love-ode,
Every song and organ mode,
Competing for a truelove,
Every catch for woman's love.
Preacher and reader of lore,
Sweet and clear, inspired rapture,
Bard of Ovid's faultless rhyme,
Chief prelate mild of Springtime.

From his birch, where lovers throng,
Author of the wood's birdsong,
Merrily the glade re-echoes –
Rhymes and metres of love he knows.
He on hazel sings so well
Through cloistered trees (winged angel)
Hardly a bird of Eden
Had by rote remembered then
How to recite what headlong
Passion made him do with song.

Dafydd ap Gwilym
(*translated from the Welsh by Tony Conran*)

Thrushes

Terrifying are the attent sleek thrushes on the lawn,
More coiled steel than living – a poised
Dark deadly eye, those delicate legs
Triggered to stirrings beyond sense – with a start, a bounce, a stab
Overtake the instant and drag out some writhing thing.
No indolent procrastinations and no yawning stares.
No sighs or head-scratchings. Nothing but bounce and stab
And a ravening second.

Is it their single-mind-sized skulls, or a trained
Body, or genius, or a nestful of brats
Gives their days this bullet and automatic
Purpose? Mozart's brain had it, and the shark's mouth
That hungers down the blood-smell even to a leak of its own
Side and devouring of itself: efficiency which
Strikes too streamlined for any doubt to pluck at it
Or obstruction deflect.

With a man it is otherwise. Heroisms on horseback,
Outstripping his desk-diary at a broad desk,
Carving at a tiny ivory ornament
For years: his act worships itself – while for him,
Though he bends to be blent in the prayer, how loud
    and above what
Furious spaces of fire do the distracting devils
Orgy and hosannah, under what wilderness
Of black silent waters weep.

Ted Hughes

Blackbird

'Sing a song of sixpence'

Sing a song of sixpence a pocket full of rye,
Four and twenty blackbirds baked in a pie.
When the pie was opened the birds began to sing,
Oh wasn't that a dainty dish to set before the king?
The king was in his counting house counting out his money,
The queen was in the parlour eating bread and honey.
The maid was in the garden hanging out the clothes,
When down came a blackbird and pecked off her nose!

Anonymous

The Blackbird

Ov' all the birds upon the wing
Between the zunny show'rs o' spring, –
Vor all the lark, a-swingèn high,
Mid zing below a cloudless sky,
An' sparrows, clust'rèn roun' the bough,
Mid chatter to the men at plough, –
The blackbird, whisslèn in among
The boughs, do zing the gaÿest zong.

Vor we do hear the blackbird zing
His sweetest ditties in the spring,
When nippèn win's noo mwore do blow
Vrom northern skies, wi' sleet or snow,

But drēve light doust along between
The leäne-zide hedges, thick an' green;
An' zoo the blackbird in among
The boughs do zing the gaÿest zong.

'Tis blithe, wi' newly-open'd eyes,
To zee the mornèn's ruddy skies;
Or, out a-haulèn frith or lops
Vrom new-plēsh'd hedge or new vell'd copse,
To rest at noon in primrwose beds
Below the white-bark'd woak trees' heads;
But there's noo time, the whole daÿ long,
Lik' evenèn wi' the blackbird's zong.

Vor when my work is all a-done
Avore the zettèn o' the zun,
Then blushèn Jeäne do walk along
The hedge to meet me in the drong,
An' staÿ till all is dim an' dark
Bezides the ashen tree's white bark;
An' all bezides the blackbird's shrill
An' runnèn evenèn-whissle's still.

An' there in bwoyhood I did rove
Wi' pryèn eycs along the drove
To vind the nest the blackbird meäde
O' grass-stalks in the high bough's sheäde:
Or clim' aloft, wi' clingèn knees,
Vor crows' aggs up in swaÿèn trees,
While frighten'd blackbirds down below
Did chatter o' their little foe.
An' zoo there's noo pleäce lik' the drong,
Where I do hear the blackbird's zong.

William Barnes

drēve, drive; *frith*, brushwood; *lops*, kindling sticks; *plēsh*, to lay a hedge by
pegging down the cut stems; *drong*, a narrow way

Adlestrop

Yes, I remember Adlestrop –
The name, because one afternoon
Of heat the express-train drew up there
Unwontedly. It was late June.

The steam hissed. Someone cleared his throat.
No one left and no one came
On the bare platform. What I saw
Was Adlestrop – only the name

And willows, willow-herb, and grass,
And meadowsweet, and haycocks dry,
No whit less still and lonely fair
Than the high cloudlets in the sky.

And for that minute a blackbird sang
Close by, and round him, mistier,
Farther and farther, all the birds
Of Oxfordshire and Gloucestershire.

                                        Edward Thomas

St Kevin and the Blackbird

And then there was St Kevin and the blackbird.
The saint is kneeling, arms stretched out, inside
His cell, but the cell is narrow, so

One turned-up palm is out the window, stiff
As a crossbeam, when a blackbird lands
And lays in it and settles down to nest.

Kevin feels the warm eggs, the small breast, the tucked
Neat head and claws and, finding himself linked
Into the network of eternal life,

Is moved to pity: now he must hold his hand
Like a branch out in the sun and rain for weeks
Until the young are hatched and fledged and flown.

★

And since the whole thing's imagined anyhow,
Imagine being Kevin. Which is he?
Self-forgetful or in agony all the time

From the neck on out down through his hurting forearms?
Are his fingers sleeping? Does he still feel his knees?
Or has the shut-eyed blank of underearth

Crept up through him? Is there distance in his head?
Alone and mirrored clear in love's deep river,
'To labour and not to seek reward,' he prays,

A prayer his body makes entirely
For he has forgotten self, forgotten bird
And on the riverbank forgotten the river's name.

Seamus Heaney

Eggs & Nests

Birds' Nests

The summer nests uncovered by autumn wind,
Some torn, others dislodged, all dark,
Everyone sees them: low or high in tree,
Or hedge, or single bush, they hang like a mark.

Since there's no need of eyes to see them with
I cannot help a little shame
That I missed most, even at eye's level, till
The leaves blew off and made the seeing no game.

'Tis a light pang. I like to see the nests
Still in their places, now first known,
At home and by far roads. Boys never found them,
Whatever jays or squirrels may have done.

And most I like the winter nest deep-hid
That leaves and berries fell into;
Once a dormouse dined there on hazel nuts;
And grass and goose-grass seeds found soil and grew.

Edward Thomas

Birds' Nests

How fresh the air the birds how busy now
In every walk if I but peep I find
Nests newly made or finished all and lined
With hair and thistle down and in the bough
Of little awthorn huddled up in green
The leaves still thickening as the spring gets age
The Pinks quite round and snug and closely laid
And linnets of materials loose and rough
And still hedge sparrow moping in the shade
Near the hedge bottom weaves of homely stuff
Dead grass and mosses green an hermitage
For secresy and shelter rightly made
And beautiful it is to walk beside
The lanes and hedges where their homes abide

John Clare

On the Spot

A cold clutch, a whole nestful, all but hidden
In last year's autumn leaf-mould, and I knew
By the mattness and the stillness of them, rotten,
Making death sweat of a morning dew
That didn't so much shine the shells as damp them.
I was down on my hands and knees there in the wet
Grass under the hedge, adoring it,
Early riser busy reaching in
And used to finding warm eggs. But instead
This sudden polar stud

And stigma and dawn stone-circle chill
In my mortified right hand, proof positive
Of what conspired on the spot to addle
Matter in its planetary stand-off.

Seamus Heaney

The Explosion

On the day of the explosion
Shadows pointed towards the pithead:
In the sun the slagheap slept.

Down the lane came men in pitboots
Coughing oath-edged talk and pipe-smoke,
Shouldering off the freshened silence.

One chased after rabbits; lost them;
Came back with a nest of lark's eggs;
Showed them; lodged them in the grasses.

So they passed in beards and moleskins,
Fathers, brothers, nicknames, laughter,
Through the tall gates standing open.

At noon, there came a tremor; cows
Stopped chewing for a second; sun,
Scarfed as in a heat-haze, dimmed.

The dead go on before us, they
Are sitting in God's house in comfort,
We shall see them face to face —

Plain as lettering in the chapels
It was said, and for a second
Wives saw men of the explosion

Larger than in life they managed –
Gold as on a coin, or walking
Somehow from the sun towards them,

One showing the eggs unbroken.

Philip Larkin

The Exposed Nest

You were forever finding some new play.
So when I saw you down on hands and knees
In the meadow, busy with the new-cut hay,
Trying, I thought, to set it up on end,
I went to show you how to make it stay,
If that was your idea, against the breeze,
And, if you asked me, even help pretend
To make it root again and grow afresh.
But 'twas no make-believe with you today,
Nor was the grass itself your real concern,
Though I found your hand full of wilted fern,
Steel-bright June-grass, and blackening heads of clover.
'Twas a nest full of young birds on the ground
The cutter bar had just gone champing over
(Miraculously without tasting flesh)
And left defenseless to the heat and light.
You wanted to restore them to their right
Of something interposed between their sight
And too much world at once – could means be found.
The way the nest-full every time we stirred

Stood up to us as to a mother-bird
Whose coming home has been too long deferred,
Made me ask would the mother-bird return
And care for them in such a change of scene,
And might our meddling make her more afraid.
That was a thing we could not wait to learn.
We saw the risk we took in doing good,
But dared not spare to do the best we could
Though harm should come of it; so built the screen
You had begun, and gave them back their shade.
All this to prove we cared. Why is there then
No more to tell? We turned to other things.
I haven't any memory – have you? –
Of ever coming to the place again
To see if the birds lived the first night through,
And so at last to learn to use their wings.

Robert Frost

Bird-nesting

As if this moment someone dropped a stone
In the new green field the splash of hawthorns grows
In sight of the farm. A boy bird-nesting waits
In a nearby hedge to retrieve the confiscated
Copse from adults to resume his primitive game.
At his approach a wood pigeon rows away;
He enters by an overhanging bough
The indoor quiet of leaves upon the ground:
Dead branches like old barbed wire protect the trees
And put restraining twigs inside his sleeves
And pockets as he climbs; halfway he uncatches
The magpie's soft explosion from its nest.
He clambers down, an egg inside his mouth,

And pricks it with a thorn and blows it out,
Guilty but exhilarated
At covering in reverse the route of creation.

Stanley Cook

Chiffchaff

The Pettichap's Nest

Well in my many walks I rarely found
A place less likely for a bird to form
Its nest close by the rut gulled waggon road
And on the almost bare foot-trodden ground
With scarce a clump of grass to keep it warm
And not a thistle spreads its spears abroad
Or prickly bush to shield it from harms way
And yet so snugly made that none may spy
It out save accident – and you and I
Had surely passed it in our walk to day
Had chance not led us by it – nay e'en now
Had not the old bird heard us trampling bye
And fluttered out – we had not seen it lie
Brown as the roadway side – small bits of hay
Pluckt from the old propt-haystacks pleachy brow
And withered leaves make up its outward walls
That from the snub-oak dotterel yearly falls
And in the old hedge bottom rot away
Built like a oven with a little hole
Hard to discover – that snug entrance wins
Scarcely admitting e'en two fingers in
And lined with feathers warm as silken stole
And soft as seats of down for painless ease
And full of eggs scarce bigger e'en then peas

Heres one most delicate with spots as small
As dust – and of a faint and pinky red
– We'll let them be and safety guard them well
For fear's rude paths around are thickly spread
And they are left to many dangers ways
When green grass hoppers jumps might break the shells
While lowing oxen pass them morn and night
And restless sheep around them hourly stray
And no grass springs but hungry horses bite
That trample past them twenty times a day
Yet like a miracle in safetys lap
They still abide unhurt and out of sight
– Stop heres the bird that woodman at the gap
Hath frit it from the hedge –tis olive green –
Well I declare it is the pettichaps
Not bigger than the wren and seldom seen:
Ive often found their nests in chances way
When I in pathless woods did idly roam
But never did I dream until today
A spot like this would be her chosen home

John Clare

Long-tailed Tit

Bumbarrel's Nest

The oddling bush, close sheltered hedge new-plashed,
Of which spring's early liking makes a guest
First with a shade of green though winter-dashed –
There, full as soon, bumbarrels make a nest
Of mosses grey with cobwebs closely tied
And warm and rich as feather-bed within,
With little hole on its contrary side
That pathway peepers may no knowledge win
Of what her little oval nest contains –
Ten eggs and often twelve, with dusts of red
Soft frittered – and full soon the little lanes
Screen the young crowd and hear the twitt'ring song
Of the old birds who call them to be fed
While down the hedge they hang and hide along.

John Clare

Chickadee

Flit

      — dart — an idea
arcs the cold, then a clutch

of related thoughts;
slim branches don't even

flicker with the weight
of what's landed;

animate alphabet
whizzing past our faces,

little black and white hurry,
as if a form of notation

accompanied our walk,
a little ahead of us

and a bit behind. If we
could *see* their trajectory,

if their trace remained
in the winter air,

what a tunnel they'd figure:
skein of quick vectors

above our head,
a fierce braid,

improvised, their decisions
– the way one makes poetry

from syntax – unpredictable, resolving
to wild regularity

(thought has to flit
to describe it, speech

has to try that hurry).
A scaffolding,

a kind of argument
about being numerous.

Thread and rethread – alight.
Study. We might be carrying

crumbs. We're not. I wish.
Their small heads cock,

they lift (no visible effort,
as if flight were the work

of the will only), light,
a little further along,

and though they're silent
it seems you could hear

the minute repeating registers
of their attention,

*_____, *_____, the *here you are*
yes here you yes.

Pronoun reference unclear.
Who looks at us

– an aerial association
of a dozen subjectivities,

or a singular self
wearing, this snowy afternoon,

twelve pair of wings?
Collectivity of sparks,

sparking collectivity? Say *live*
resides not inside feathers or skin

but in the whizzing medium.
No third person.

Sharp, clear globe of January,
and we – the fourteen of us –

the thinking taking place.
We is instances of alertness,

grammar help me.
Mind in the ringing day,

a little of us ahead
and a bit behind,

and all that action
barely disturbs the air.

Mark Doty

Shrike

The Shrike

When night comes black
Such royal dreams beckon this man
As lift him apart
From his earth-wife's side
To wing, sleep-feathered,
The singular air,
While she, envious bride,
Cannot follow after, but lies
With her blank brown eyes starved wide,
Twisting curses in the tangled sheet
With taloned fingers,
Shaking in her skull's cage
The stuffed shape of her flown mate
Escaped among moon-plumaged strangers;
So hungered, she must wait in rage
Until bird-racketing dawn
When her shrike-face
Leans to peck open those locked lids, to eat
Crowns, palace, all
That nightlong stole her male,
And with red beak
Spike and suck out
Last blood-drop of that truant heart.

Sylvia Plath

American Crow

To Victor Hugo of My Crow Pluto

'Even when the bird is walking we know that it has wings.'
    – Victor Hugo

Of:
    my crow
    Pluto,

    the true
    Plato,

    azzurro-
    negro

    green-blue
    rainbow –

    Victor Hugo,
    it is true

    we know
    that the crow

    'has wings,' how-
    ever pigeon-toe-

225

inturned on grass. We do.
  (adagio)

Vivo-
rosso

'corvo,'
although

con dizio-
nario

io parlo
Italiano –

this pseudo
Esperanto

which, savio
ucello

you speak too –
my vow and motto

(botto e totto)
io giuro

è questo
credo:

lucro
è peso morto.

And so
dear crow –

gioièllo
mio –

I have to
let you go;

a bel bosco
generoso,

tuttuto
vagabondo,

serafino
uvaceo

Sunto,
oltremarino

verecondo
Plato, addio.

Impromptu equivalents for *esperanto madinusa* (made in U.S.A.) for
those who might not resent them.

azzurro-negro: blue-black
vivorosso: lively
con dizionario: with dictionary
savio ucello: knowing bird
botto e totto: vow and motto
io giuro: I swear
è questo credo: is this credo
lucro è peso morto: profit is a
    dead weight

gioièllo mio: my jewel
a bel bosco: to lovely woods
tuttuto vagabondo: complete
    gypsy
serafino uvaceo: grape-black
    seraph
sunto: in short
verecondo: modest

Marianne Moore

Crows on the North Slope

When the Gentle were dead these inherited their coats
Now they gather in late autumn and quarrel over the air
Demanding something for their shadows that are naked
And silent and learning

W. S. Merwin

My Crow

A crow flew into the tree outside my window.
It was not Ted Hughes's crow, or Galway's crow.
Or Frost's, Pasternak's, or Lorca's crow.
Or one of Homer's crows, stuffed with gore,
after the battle. This was just a crow.
That never fit in anywhere in its life,
or did anything worth mentioning.
It sat there on the branch for a few minutes.
Then picked up and flew beautifully
out of my life.

Raymond Carver

Carrion Crow

Sonnet: The Crow

How peaceable it seems for lonely men
To see a crow fly in the thin blue line
Over the woods and fields, o'er level fen
It speaks of villages or cottage nigh
Behind the neighbouring woods – when march winds
   high
Tear off the branches of the huge old oak
I love to see these chimney sweeps sail by
And hear them o'er the gnarlèd forest croak
Then sosh askew from the hid woodmans stroke
That in the woods their daily labours ply.
I love the sooty crow nor would provoke
Its march day exercise of croaking joy
I love to see it sailing to and fro
While feelds, and woods and waters spread below

John Clare

Song

Old Adam, the carrion crow,
   The old crow of Cairo;
He sat in the shower, and let it flow
   Under his tail and over his crest;

And through every feather
Leaked the wet weather;
And the bough swung under his nest;
For his beak it was heavy with marrow.
  Is that the wind dying? O no;
  It's only two devils, that blow
  Through a murderer's bones, to and fro,
    In the ghosts' moonshine.

Ho! Eve, my grey carrion wife,
  When we have supped on kings' marrow,
Where shall we drink and make merry our life?
  Our nest it is queen Cleopatra's skull,
    'Tis cloven and cracked,
    And battered and hacked,
  But with tears of blue eyes it is full:
  Let us drink then, my raven of Cairo.
    Is that the wind dying? O no;
    It's only two devils, that blow
    Through a murderer's bones, to and fro,
      In the ghosts' moonshine.

                              Thomas Lovell Beddoes

Crow and the Birds

When the eagle soared clear through a dawn distilling of emerald
When the curlew trawled in seadusk through a chime of
    wineglasses
When the swallow swooped through a woman's song in a cavern
And the swift flicked through the breath of a violet

When the owl sailed clear of tomorrow's conscience
And the sparrow preened himself of yesterday's promise
And the heron laboured clear of the Bessemer upglare
And the bluetit zipped clear of lace panties
And the woodpecker drummed clear of the rotovator and the
    rose-farm
And the peewit tumbled clear of the laundromat

While the bullfinch plumped in the apple bud
And the goldfinch bulbed in the sun
And the wryneck crooked in the moon
And the dipper peered from the dewball

Crow spraddled head-down in the beach-garbage, guzzling a
    dropped ice-cream.

                               Ted Hughes

A Crow's Skull

found beside the railway line
and bleached in a tin

then sent to you
before I knew

the trouble we were in
this skull like a ring

is the least it can be
and all its candour

comes from what's lost
what's no more and is not

as mine does
now I speak of us

Jacob Polley

Rook

February Dawn

Rooks flew across the sky, bright February watched
Their steady course straight on, like an etcher's line scratched.
The dark brown or tawny earth breathed incense up,
I guessed there were hidden daisies, hoped the first buttercup.

The tunes of all the county, old-fashioned and my own
Wilful, wanton, careless, thronged in my mind, alone.
The sight of earth and rooks made passion rise in my blood.
Far gleamed Cotswold. Near ran Severn. A god's mood.

Save that I knew no high things would amaze day-fall
I had prayed heaven to kill me at that time most to fulfil
My dreams for ever. But looked on to a west bright at five,
Scarred by rooks in purpose; and the late trees in strife.

Ivor Gurney

Black Rook in Rainy Weather

On the stiff twig up there
Hunches a wet black rook
Arranging and rearranging its feathers in the rain.
I do not expect miracle
Or an accident

To set the sight on fire
In my eye, nor seek
Any more in the desultory weather some design,
But let spotted leaves fall as they fall,
Without ceremony, or portent.

Although, I admit, I desire,
Occasionally, some backtalk
From the mute sky, I can't honestly complain:
A certain minor light may still
Leap incandescent

Out of kitchen table or chair
As if a celestial burning took
Possession of the most obtuse objects now and then –
Thus hallowing an interval
Otherwise inconsequent

By bestowing largesse, honour,
One might say love. At any rate, I now walk
Wary (for it could happen
Even in this dull, ruinous landscape); sceptical,
Yet politic; ignorant

Of whatever angel may choose to flare
Suddenly at my elbow. I only know that a rook
Ordering its black feathers can so shine
As to seize my sense, haul
My eyelids up, and grant

A brief respite from fear
Of total neutrality. With luck,
Trekking stubborn through this season
Of fatigue, I shall
Patch together a content

Of sorts. Miracles occur,
If you care to call those spasmodic
Tricks of radiance miracles. The wait's begun again,
The long wait for the angel,
For that rare, random descent.

Sylvia Plath

Magpie

Magpie

'Good morning, Mr Magpie. How's your wife
Today?' I say. Spit on the risky air
Three times. The domino-coloured bird skips off
Through lodgepole pines, dry leaves of aspen poplar
Crisping the path.
            You throw your head back, wear
For a splinter of time my hand in yours, and laugh
Aloud. And suddenly you say, 'You know
Aspen and poplar are the first to grow
After a fire?'
           The Celt in me, unsafe
Before the magic bird, is hauling up
A rhyme from childhood. *One for sorrow, two*
For mirth. Three for a wedding . . . 'Magot pies'
Macbeth called them: they point out murderers,
Whose touch makes murdered blood flare out again.

The sun swims down the altered mountain; roughs
A gold line round your head. A wail of box-
Cars threads the valley as I try to scrape
My hand of blood, watching the magpie's track.
He struts in the dust. Bullies a whisky jack.

Charles Causley

NOTE: *whisky jack*: Canadian common grey jay

236

Raven

from Noah's Ark

Then, as the lifted land lay upwards,
Where the wind and weather warped it,
The ark upon a soft day, settled to the ground,
By a raised up rock, rested it at last,
On the mount of Marrach, on the Armerne hills
Waft Noe his window wide, and wised thereout;
Sought the service of his servants, the earth to seek,
Remembered he the raven, (rank rebel Raven!
O Coloured as a coal! O crow untrue!)
Flaps he into flight, fanning on the wind,
High is he upon his heart, to hearken tidings!
Croaks he for comfort, for carrion he finds,
For cast upon the cliffs the rotting corpses lay.
He smelt the stench, and sought them,
Fell upon the foul flesh, filling full his belly,
Full soon, slips yesterday's strife and storm,
Forgotten his captain's charges, left in the coffer,
The raven recking forth, recks he very little
How all other fare, if he findeth meat!

Anonymous

The Twa Corbies

As I was walking all alane,
I heard twa corbies making a mane;
The tane unto the t'other say,
'Where sall we gang and dine to-day?'

'– In behint yon auld fail dyke,
I wot there lies a new slain Knight;
And naebody kens that he lies there,
But his hawk, his hound, and lady fair.

'His hound is to the hunting gane,
His hawk to fetch the wild-fowl hame,
His lady's ta'en another mate,
So we may mak our dinner sweet.

'Ye'll sit on his white hause-bane,
And I'll pike out his bonny blue een;
Wi ae lock o his gowden hair
We'll theek our nest when it grows bare.

'Mony a one for him makes mane,
But nane sall ken where he is gane;
Oer his white banes, when they are bare,
The wind sall blaw for evermair.'

Anonymous

The Ravens Nest

Upon the collar of an hugh old oak
Year after year boys mark a curious nest
Of twigs made up a faggot near in size
And boys to reach it try all sorts of schemes
But not a twig to reach with hand or foot
Sprouts from the pillared trunk and as to try
To swarm the massy bulk tis all in vain
They scarce one effort make to hitch them up
But down they sluther soon as ere they try
So long hath been their dwelling there – old men
When passing bye will laugh and tell the ways
They had when boys to climb that very tree
And as it so would seem that very nest
That ne'er was missing from that self same spot
A single year in all their memorys
And they will say that the two birds are now
The very birds that owned the dwelling then
Some think it strange yet certaintys at loss
And cannot contradict it so they pass
As old birds living the woods patriarchs
Old as the oldest men so famed and known
That even men will thirst into the fame
Of boys at get at schemes that now and then
May captivate a young one from the tree
With iron claums and bands adventuring up
The mealy trunk or else by waggon ropes
Slung over the hugh grains and so drawn up
By those at bottom one assends secure
With foot rope stirruped – still a perrilous way
So perrilous that one and only one
In memorys of the oldest men was known
To wear his boldness to intentions end
And reach the ravens nest – and thence acchieved

A theme that wonder treasured for supprise
By every cottage hearth the village through
Not yet forgot though other darers come
With daring times that scale the steeples top
And tye their kerchiefs to the weather cock
As trophys that the dangerous deed was done
Yet even now in these adventureous days
No one is bold enough to dare the way
Up the old monstrous oak where every spring
Finds the two ancient birds at their old task
Repairing the hugh nest – where still they live
Through changes winds and storms and are secure
And like a landmark in the chronicles
Of village memorys treasured up yet lives
The hugh old oak that wears the ravens nest

John Clare

Jackdaw

The Jack Daw

There is a bird who by his coat,
And by the hoarseness of his note,
　　Might be suppos'd a crow;
A great frequenter of the church,
Where bishop-like he finds a perch,
　　And dormitory too.

Above the steeple shines a plate,
That turns and turns, to indicate
　　From what point blows the weather;
Look up – your brains begin to swim,
'Tis in the clouds – that pleases him,
　　He chooses it the rather.

Fond of the speculative height,
Thither he wings his airy flight,
　　And thence securely sees
The bustle and the raree-show
That occupy mankind below,
　　Secure and at his ease.

You think no doubt he sits and muses
On future broken bones and bruises,
    If he should chance to fall;
No not a single thought like that
Employs his philosophic pate,
    Or troubles it at all.

He sees that this great roundabout
The world, with all its motley rout,
    Church, army, physic, law,
Its customs and its businesses
Are no concern at all of his,
    And says, what says he? Caw.

Thrice happy bird! I too have seen
Much of the vanities of men,
    And sick of having seen 'em,
Would chearfully these limbs resign
For such a pair of wings as thine,
    And such a head between 'em.

                                William Cowper

Blue Jay

The Blue Jay

The blue jay with a crest on his head
Comes round the cabin in the snow.
He runs in the snow like a bit of blue metal,
Turning his back on everything.

From the pine-tree that towers and hisses like a pillar of shaggy
        cloud
Immense above the cabin
Comes a strident laugh as we approach, this little black dog
        and I.
So halts the little black bitch on four spread paws in the snow
And looks up inquiringly into the pillar of cloud,
With a tinge of misgiving.
Ca-a-a! comes the scrape of ridicule out of the tree.

What voice of the Lord is that, from the tree of smoke?

Oh, Bibbles, little black bitch in the snow,
With a pinch of snow in the groove of your silly snub nose,
What do you look at *me* for?
What do you look at me for, with such misgiving?

It's the blue jay laughing at us.
It's the blue jay jeering at us, Bibs.

Every day since the snow is here
The blue jay paces round the cabin, very busy, picking up bits,
Turning his back on us all,
And bobbing his thick dark crest about the snow, as if darkly
        saying:
I ignore those folk who look out.

You acid-blue metallic bird,
You thick bird with a strong crest,

Who are you?
Whose boss are you, with all your bully way?
You copper-sulphate blue bird!

D. H. Lawrence

Starling

Starlings Have Come

A horde out of sub-Arctic Asia
Darkening nightfall, a faint sky-roar
Of pressure on the ear.

More thicken the vortex, gloomier.

A bacteria cyclone, a writhing of imps
Issuing from a hole in the horizon
Topples and blackens a whole farm.

Now a close-up seething of fleas.
                    And now a silence —
The doom-panic mob listens, for a second.
Then, with a soft boom, they wrap you
Into their mind-warp, assembling a nightmare sky-wheel
Of escape — a Niagara
Of upward rumbling wings — that collapses again

In an unmanageable weight
Of neurotic atoms.
                They're the subconscious
Of the Smart-Alec, all slick hair and Adam's apple,
Sunday chimney starling.
                    This Elizabethan songster,
Italianate, in damask, emblematic,
Trembles his ruff, pierces the Maytime

With his perfected whistle
Of a falling bomb – or frenzies himself
Into a Gothic, dishevelled madness,
Chattering his skeleton, sucking his brains,
Gargling his blood through a tin flute –

                        Ah, Shepster!
Suddenly such a bare dagger of listening!

Next thing – down at the bread
Screeching like a cat
Limber and saurian on your hind legs,

Tumbling the sparrows with a drop kick –

A Satanic hoodlum, a cross-eyed boss,
Black body crammed with hot rubies
And Anthrax under your nails.

                            Ted Hughes

Mimics

These April dawns when brimming gutters flick
Frayed threads of water out on windy air,
Under the eaves or up the chimney stack
The starlings perform their borrowed repertoire.

Here, iambic, urgent, minatory,
The moorhen drives her young into the reeds;
There, bansheeing phantoms of the sky,
The Canada geese fletch rippling arrowheads.

Each copied sound has had to be reduced
To fit their marginal remote domain:
I have heard even our dog's bark reproduced
In thin-toned miniature; and a jet plane

246

Will sometimes whine softly over the tiles.
And yet, though not supposing these mimics mean
To choose their sounds of mopeds, lambs and owls,
Or that such random echoes mask design,

How, waking with words half dead on the tongue,
Can I not admire this power they command
To mould, with meek precision, a sort of song
Out of what's stolen, lost or secondhand?

David Hartnett

The Flock in the Firth

As Eh cam owre thi Forth rail brig
Eh saw frae oot o Fife
a farrachin o starlins, trig
as thi thochts o ane waukrife.

Lyk sheelock fae a thrashin mill
they mirlieit thi nicht
atween thi brigs, as tho tae fill ut
wi wan shammade o flicht.

Lyk a sark that's bealin i thi breeze
this ram stam scarnach oan
a norrie birled wi siccan ease
assa skatir by'ur lone.

---

farrachin: bustling; *waukrife*: unable to sleep; *sheelock*: chaff; *mirlieit*: speckled;
shammade: lacework; *sark*: shirt; *bealin*: moving agitatedly; *ram stam*: head-
strong; *scarnach*: great number of people or things; *norrie*: whim; *birld*; spun;
by'ur lone: by herself

Ut seemd as tho a michty scroosh
o sparlins fae thi flair
o Forth hud fur a skirr gaed whoosh
intil thi deeps o air.

Ut seemd as tho a page o wurds
at sum parafflin nemm,
had aa at wance been cheengd tae burds
an werr marginin thi faem.

Thi mirk held mair nor myriads
aa sherrickin thi stream,
in spirlin splores, in sklents, in scads,
lyk Hitchcock's wuddendreme.

Lyk Egypt's *kas*, or Dante's braw
adulterers in Hell,
sae mony starlins i thi blaw
o Scoatlan rose an fell.

Eh slid ablow thi skavie flock
and oantae Fife's blank page,
Eh wrote: they are thi parrymauk
o starnies inna rage.

W. S. Herbert

scroosh: disreputable horde; *sparlin*: smelt (a freshwater fish found in the Forth
and the Tay); *skirr*: jape; *parafflin*: flourishing, as at the end of a signature;
marginin: marking the margin; *mirk*: dark; *sherrickin*: amassing to abuse;
spirlin splores: lively excursions; *sklents*: angles; *scads*: in great quantities;
wuddendreme: nightmare; *skavie*: rushing; *parrymauk*: double; *starnies*: stars
('starn' also means 'starling')

Deaths & Depletions 4

Proud Songsters

The thrushes sing as the sun is going,
And the finches whistle in ones and pairs,
And as it gets dark loud nightingales
    In bushes
Pipe, as they can when April wears,
    As if all Time were theirs.

These are brand-new birds of twelve-months' growing,
Which a year ago, or less than twain,
No finches were, nor nightingales,
    Nor thrushes,
But only particles of grain,
    And earth, and air, and rain.

Thomas Hardy

Perfect

On the Western Seaboard of South Uist
Los muertos abren los ojos a los que viven

I found a pigeon's skull on the machair,
All the bones pure white and dry, and chalky,
But perfect,
Without a crack or a flaw anywhere.

At the back, rising out of the beak,
Were domes like bubbles of thin bone,
Almost transparent, where the brain had been
That fixed the tilt of the wings.

Hugh MacDiarmid

On a Bird Dead in the Road

What formerly flounced and flew its fantastic feathers
Now lies like a flattened old leather glove in the road,
And the gigantic wheels of the articulated juggernaut lorries
Pound down on it all day long like the mad will of god.

George Barker

Blackbird

On our side of the glass
You laid out the blackbird's
Sleepy eyes, its twiggy
Toes, crisp tail-feathers
And its wings wider than
The light from two windows.

Michael Longley

House Sparrow

The Dead Sparrow

Tell me not of joy; there's none,
Now my little Sparrow's gone:
   He, just as you,
   Would try and woo,
He would chirp and flatter me;
He would hang the wing awhile –
Till at length he saw me smile.
Lord, how sullen he would be!

He would catch a crumb, and then
Sporting, let it go agen;
   He from my lip
   Would moisture sip;
He would from my trencher feed;
Then would hop, and then would run,
And cry *Philip* when he'd done.
O! whose heart can choose but bleed?

O how eager would he fight,
And ne'er hurt, though he did bite.
   Nor morn did pass,
   But on my glass
He would sit, and mark and do
What I did – now ruffle all
His feathers o'er, now let 'em fall;
And then straightway sleek them too.

Whence will Cupid get his darts
Feathered now to pierce our hearts?
  A wound he may
  Not, Love, convey,

Now this faithful bird is gone;
  O let mournful turtles join
  With loving red-breasts, and combine
To sing dirges o'er his stone!

                 William Cartwright

Mr and Mrs Spikky Sparrow

On a little piece of wood,
Mr Spikky Sparrow stood;
Mrs Sparrow sate close by,
A-making of an insect pie,
For her little children five,
In the nest and all alive,
Singing with a cheerful smile
To amuse them all while,
  Twikky wikky wikky wee,
  Wikky bikky twikky tee,
    Spikky bikky bee!

Mrs Spikky Sparrow said,
'Spikky, Darling! in my head
Many thoughts of trouble come,
Like to flies upon a plum!
All last night, among the trees,
I heard you cough, I heard you sneeze;
And, thought I, it's come to that
Because he does not wear a hat!
    Chippy wippy sikky tee!
    Bikky wikky tikky mee!
        Spikky chippy wee!

'Not that you are growing old,
But the nights are growing cold.
No one stays out all night long
Without a hat: I'm sure it's wrong!'
Mr Spikky said, 'How kind,
Dear! you are! to speak your mind!
All your life I wish you luck!
You are! you are! a lovely duck!
    Witchy witchy witchy wee!
    Twitchy witchy witchy bee!
        Tikky tikky tee!

'I was also sad, and thinking,
When one day I saw you winking,
And I heard you sniffle-snuffle,
And I saw your feathers ruffle;
To myself I sadly said,
She's neuralgia in her head!
That dear head has nothing on it!
Ought she not to wear a bonnet?
    Witchy kitchy kitchy wee?
    Spikky wikky mikky bee?
        Chippy wippy chee?

'Let us both fly up to town!
There I'll buy you such a gown!
Which, completely in the fashion,
You shall tie a sky-blue sash on.
And a pair of slippers neat,
To fit your darling little feet,
So that you will look and feel
Quite galloobious and genteel!
  Jikky wikky bikky see,
    Chicky bikky wikky bee,
      Twicky witchy wee!'

So they both to London went,
Alighting on the Monument,
Whence they flew down swiftly – pop,
Into Moses' wholesale shop;
There they bought a hat and bonnet,
And a gown with spots upon it,
A satin sash of Cloxam blue,
And a pair of slippers too.
  Zikky wikky mikky bee,
    Witchy witchy mitchy kee,
      Sikky tikky wee!

Then when so completely drest,
Back they flew, and reached their nest.
Their children cried, 'O Ma and Pa!
How truly beautiful you are!'

254

Said they, 'We trust that cold or pain
We shall never feel again!
While, perched on tree, or house, or steeple,
We now shall look like other people.
   Witchy witchy witchy wee,
   Twikky mikky bikky bee,
      Zikky sikky tee!'

                                        Edward Lear

House Sparrows

The sparrows have quit our house, house sparrows
That cheeped in the gutters, stone-age hangers-on
That splashed in our puddles, dust-bathers.
                                        'Yea,
The sparrow hath found her an house.' But where?

Carthorses are munching oats from their nosebags
At a water trough surrounded by sparrows
That bicker and pick up the falling grains.

                                        Michael Longley

For the House Sparrow, in Decline

Your numbers fall and it's tempting to think
you're deserting our suburbs and estates
like your cousins at Pompeii; that when you return
to bathe in dust and build your nests again
in a roofless world where no one hears your *cheeps*,
only a starling's modem mimicry
will remind you of how you once supplied
the incidental music of our lives.

Paul Farley

Sparrow

*If a sparrow come before my window I take part in its existence
and pick about the gravel.*
    John Keats to Benjamin Bailey, 22 November 1817

No longer
country clubber,
barn bouncer,
hedgerow flasher,
bran dipper,
puddle bather,
dust bowler,
stubble scrounger,
dew nibbler,
creeper sleeper,
dung dobbler.
No longer
city slicker,
curb crawler,

gutter weaver,
brick clinger,
dotty mobster,
sill scruffer,
traffic dodger,
drain clogger,
putty pecker,
car bomber.
No longer
daily greeter,
scratch singer,
piebald shitter,
bib bobber,
cocky bugger,
boss brawler,
gossip spinner,
crowd pleaser,
heaven filler,
wing dancer.
No longer.

Andrew Motion

Bullfinch

On the Death of
Mrs Throckmorton's Bulfinch (1788)

Ye nymphs! if e'er your eyes were red
With tears o'er hapless fav'rites shed,
 O share Maria's grief!
Her fav'rite, even in his cage,
(What will not hunger's cruel rage?)
 Assassin'd by a thief.

Where Rhenus strays his vines among,
The egg was laid from which he sprung,
 And though by nature mute,
Or only with a whistle blest,
Well-taught, he all the sounds express'd
 Of flagelet or flute.

The honours of his ebon poll
Were brighter than the sleekest mole;
 His bosom of the hue
With which Aurora decks the skies,
When piping winds shall soon arise
 To sweep up all the dew.

Above, below, in all the house,
Dire foe, alike to bird and mouse,
　　No cat had leave to dwell;
And Bully's cage supported stood,
On props of smoothest-shaven wood,
　　Large-built and lattic'd well.

Well-lattic'd – but the grate, alas!
Not rough with wire of steel or brass,
　　For Bully's plumage sake,
But smooth with wands from Ouse's side,
With which, when neatly peel'd and dried,
　　The swains their baskets make.

Night veil'd the pole – all seem'd secure –
When led by instinct sharp and sure,
　　Subsistence to provide,
A beast forth sallied on the scout,
Long-back'd, long-tail'd, with whisker'd snout,
　　And badger-colour'd hide.

He, ent'ring at the study door,
Its ample area 'gan to explore;
　　And something in the wind
Conjectur'd, sniffing round and round,
Better than all the books he found,
　　Food, chiefly, for the mind.

Just then, by adverse fate impress'd,
A dream disturb'd poor Bully's rest;
　　In sleep he seem'd to view
A rat, fast-clinging to the cage,
And, screaming at the sad presage,
　　Awoke and found it true.

For, aided both by ear and scent,
Right to his mark the monster went –
    Ah, Muse! forbear to speak
Minute the horrors that ensued;
His teeth were strong, the cage was wood –
    He left poor Bully's beak.

He left it – but he should have ta'en
That beak, when issued many a strain
    Of such mellifluous tone,
Might have repaid him well, I wote,
For silencing so sweet a throat,
    Fast set within his own.

Maria weeps – The Muses mourn –
So, when by Bacchanalians torn,
    On Thracian Hebrus' side
The tree-enchanter Orpheus fell;
His head alone remain'd to tell
    The cruel death he died.

                              William Cowper

Goldfinch

The Caged Goldfinch

Within a churchyard, on a recent grave,
    I saw a little cage
That jailed a goldfinch. All was silence save
    Its hops from stage to stage.

There was inquiry in its wistful eye,
    And once it tried to sing;
Of him or her who placed it there, and why,
    No one knew anything.

Thomas Hardy

Greenfinch

The Green Linnet

Beneath these fruit tree boughs that shed
Their snow-white blossoms on my head,
With brightest sunshine round me spread
    Of spring's unclouded weather,
In this sequestered nook how sweet
To sit upon my orchard-seat!
And birds and flowers once more to greet,
    My last year's friends together.

One have I marked, the happiest guest
In all this covert of the blest:
Hail to thee, far above the rest
    In joy of voice and pinion!
Thou, linnet! in thy green array,
Presiding spirit here today,
Dost lead the revels of the May;
    And this is thy dominion.

While birds, and butterflies, and flowers,
Make all one band of paramours,
Thou, ranging up and down the bowers,
    Art sole in thy employment:
A life, a presence like the air,
Scattering thy gladness without care,
Too blest with any one to pair;
    Thyself thy own enjoyment.

Amid yon tuft of hazel trees,
That twinkle to the gusty breeze,
Behold him perched in ecstasies,
    Yet seeming still to hover;
There! where the flutter of his wings
Upon his back and body flings
Shadows and sunny glimmerings,
    That cover him all over.

My dazzled sight he oft deceives,
A brother of the dancing leaves;
Then flits, and from the cottage-eaves
    Pours forth his song in gushes;
As if by that exulting strain
He mocked and treated with disdain
The voiceless form he chose to feign,
    While fluttering in the bushes.

William Wordsworth

Siskin

Siskin

(Glasgow, 1967)

Small bird with green plumage,
yellow to green to white
on the underparts, yes, a siskin
alive on my own cedar,
winter visitor, resident in Scotland,
wholly himself.

I saw him, and you, too,
alive again,
thin but expert, seated
with your bird–glasses, bird book
and concentrated expression,
hoping for siskins in Vermont.

He pleased me for your sake –
not so much as he would have pleased you.
Unless it was you he came for,
and I something you inhabited
from the second his green flame
flickered in that black tree
to the next second when he was gone.

Anne Stevenson

Snow Bunting

Snow Bunting

for Sarah

At Allaran, the otters' rock, between the breakers'
Uninterrupted rummaging and – from the duach –
Larksong, I mistake your voice for your mother's voice
Deciphering otter prints long before you were born

As though you were conceived in a hayfield so small
Stone walls surrounded a single stook, and the snow
Bunting's putative tinkle from beyond the ridge
Sounded even closer than the spindrift's whispering.

Michael Longley

Yellowhammer

The Yellowhammer's Nest

Just by the wooden brig a bird flew up
Frit by the cowboy as he scrambled down
To reach the misty dewberry – let us stoop
And seek its nest – the brook we need not dread
Tis scarcely deep enough a bee to drown
So it sings harmless oer its pebbly bed
– Ay here it is stuck close beside the bank
Beneath the bunch of grass that spindles rank
Its husk seeds tall and high – tis rudely planned
Of bleached stubbles and the withered fare
That last years harvest left upon the land
Lined thinly with the horses sable hair
Five eggs pen-scribbled oer with ink their shells
Resembling writing scrawls which fancy reads
As natures poesy and pastoral spells –
They are the yellow hammers and she dwells
A poet-like – where brooks and flowery weeds
As sweet as Castaly to fancy seems
And that old molehill like as parnass hill
On which her partner haply sits and dreams
O er all her joys of song – so leave it still
A happy home of sunshine flowers and streams
Yet in the sweetest places cometh ill
A noisome weed that burthens every soil
For snakes are known with chill and deadly coil
To watch such nests and seize the helpless young

And like as though the plague became a guest
Leaving a houseless-home, a ruined nest
And mournful hath the little warbler sung
When such like woes hath rent its little breast

John Clare

The Yellowhammer

When shall I see the white thorn leaves again
And yellowhammers gath'ring the dry bents
By the Dyke side on stilly moor or fen
Feathered wi' love and nature's good intents
Rude is the nest this Architect invents,
Rural the place wi cart ruts by dyke side
Dead grass, horse hair and downy-headed bents
Tied to dead thistles she doth well provide
Close to a hill o' ants where cowslips bloom
And shed o'er meadows far their sweet perfume
In early Spring when winds blow chilly cold
The yellow hammer trailing grass will come
To fix a place and choose an early home
With yellow breast and head of solid gold

John Clare

Ovenbird

The Oven Bird

There is a singer everyone has heard,
Loud, a mid-summer and a mid-wood bird,
Who makes the solid tree trunks sound again.
He says that leaves are old and that for flowers
Mid-summer is to spring as one to ten.
He says the early petal-fall is past,
When pear and cherry bloom went down in showers
On sunny days a moment overcast;
And comes that other fall we name the fall.
He says the highway dust is over all.
The bird would cease and be as other birds
But that he knows in singing not to sing.
The question that he frames in all but words
Is what to make of a diminished thing.

Robert Frost

Oriole

'To hear an Oriole sing'

To hear an Oriole sing
May be a common thing –
Or only a divine.

It is not of the Bird
Who sings the same, unheard,
As unto Crowd –

The Fashion of the Ear
Attireth that it hear
In Dun, or fair –

So whether it be Rune,
Or whether it be none
Is of within.

The 'Tune is in the Tree –'
The Skeptic – showeth me –
'No Sir! In Thee!'

Emily Dickinson

The Orioles

What time the orioles came flying
Back to the homes, over the silvery dikes and seas,
The sad spring melted at a leap,
The shining clouds came over the hills to meet them.

The old house guards its memories, the birds
Stream over coloured snow in summer
Or back into the magic rising sun in winter.
They cluster at the feeding station, and rags of song

Greet the neighbours. 'Was that your voice?'
And in spring the mad caroling continues long after
    day-light
As each builds his hanging nest
Of pliant twigs and the softest moss and grasses.

But one morning you get up and the vermilion-coloured
Messenger is there, bigger than life at the window.
'I take my leave of you; now I fly away
To the sunny reeds and marshes of my winter home.'
And that night you gaze moodily
At the moonlit apple-blossoms, for of course
Horror and repulsion do exist! They do! And you
    wonder,
How long will the perfumed dung, the sunlit clouds
    cover my heart?

And then some morning when the snow is flying
Or it lines the black fir-trees, the light cries,
The excited songs start up in the yard!
The feeding station is glad to receive its guests,

But how long can the stopover last?
The cold begins when the last song retires,
And even when they fly against the trees in bright
   formation
You know the peace they brought was long overdue.

John Ashbery

Red-winged Blackbird

Thirteen Ways of Looking at a Blackbird

I

Among twenty snowy mountains
The only moving thing
Was the eye of the blackbird.

II

I was of three minds,
Like a tree
In which there are three blackbirds.

III

The blackbird whirled in the autumn winds.
It was a small part of the pantomime.

IV

A man and a woman
Are one.
A man and a woman and a blackbird
Are one.

V

I do not know which to prefer,
The beauty of inflexions
Or the beauty of innuendos,
The blackbird whistling
Or just after.

VI

Icicles filled the long window
With barbaric glass.
The shadow of the blackbird
Crossed it, to and fro.
The mood
Traced in the shadow
An indecipherable cause.

VII

O thin men of Haddam,
Why do you imagine golden birds?
Do you not see how the blackbird
Walks around the feet
Of the women about you?

VIII

I know noble accents
And lucid, inescapable rhythms;
But I know, too,
That the blackbird is involved
In what I know.

IX

When the blackbird flew out of sight,
It marked the edge
Of one of many circles.

X

At the sight of blackbirds
Flying in a green light
Even the bawds of euphony
Would cry out sharply.

XI

He rode over Connecticut
In a glass coach.
Once, a fear pierced him,
In that he mistook
The shadow of his equipage
For blackbirds.

XII

The river is moving.
The blackbird must be flying.

XIII

It was evening all afternoon.
It was snowing
And it was going to snow.
The blackbird sat
In the cedar limbs.

Wallace Stevens

Phoenix

A Bird Came Down the Walk

A Bird came down the Walk –
He did not know I saw –
He bit an Angleworm in halves
And ate the fellow, raw.

And then he drank a Dew
From a convenient Grass –
And then hopped sidewise to the Wall
To let a Beetle pass –

He glanced with rapid eyes
That hurried all around –
They looked like frightened Beads, I thought –
He stirred his Velvet Head

Like one in danger, Cautious,
I offered him a Crumb
And he unrolled his feathers
And rowed him softer home –

Than Oars divide the Ocean,
Too silver for a seam –
Or Butterflies, off Banks of Noon
Leap, plashless as they swim.

Emily Dickinson

The Nowhere Birds

In past centuries it was believed that
migrating birds would winter on the moon

There is no leaving for them
in such shifts south,

best weather is their territory,
their existence its insects

swallowed like distance.
For us, just a surging

of sky-piercing shapes,
pointed birds in search of moon-food,

and the weighty northern day
bereft. But from these beliefs

and from their visiting wings'
return were angels made.

Caitríona O'Reilly

A Seagull Murmur

is what they called it,
shaking their heads
like trawlermen;

276

the mewling sound of a leaking heart
        the sound
of a gull trapped in his chest.

To let it out
they ran a cut down his belly
like a fish, his open ribs

the ribs of a boat;
        and they closed him,
wired him shut.

Caulked and sea-worthy now
with his new valve; its metal
tapping away:

the dull clink
        of a signal-buoy
or a beak at the bars of a cage.

                              Robin Robertson

The Sea Bird

Walking along beside the beach
where the Mediterranean turns in sleep
under the cliffs' demiarch

through a curtain of thought I see
a dead bird and a live bird
the dead eyeless, but with a bright eye

the live bird discovered me
and stepped from a black rock into the air –
I turn from the dead bird to watch him fly,

electric, brilliant blue,
beneath he is orange, like flame,
colours I can't believe are so,

as legendary flowers bloom
incendiary in tint, so swift he
searches about the sky for room,

towering like the cliffs of this coast
with his stiletto wing
and orange on his breast:

he has consumed and drained
the colours of the sea
and the yellow of this tidal ground

till he escapes the eye, or is a ghost
and in a moment has come down
crept into the dead bird, ceased to exist.

Keith Douglas

The Unknown Bird

Three lovely notes he whistled, too soft to be heard
If others sang; but others never sang
In the great beech-wood all that May and June.
No one saw him: I alone could hear him
Though many listened. Was it but four years
Ago? or five? He never came again.

Oftenest when I heard him I was alone,
Nor could I ever make another hear.
La-la-la! he called, seeming far-off –
As if a cock crowed past the edge of the world,
As if the bird or I were in a dream.
Yet that he travelled through the trees and sometimes
Neared me, was plain, though somehow distant still
He sounded. All the proof is – I told men
What I had heard.

                  I never knew a voice,
Man, beast, or bird, better than this. I told
The naturalists; but neither had they heard
Anything like the notes that did so haunt me
I had them clear by heart and have them still.
Four years, or five, have made no difference. Then
As now that La-la-la! was bodiless sweet:
Sad more than joyful it was, if I must say
That it was one or other, but if sad
'Twas sad only with joy too, too far off
For me to taste it. But I cannot tell
If truly never anything but fair
The days were when he sang, as now they seem.
This surely I know, that I who listened then,
Happy sometimes, sometimes suffering
A heavy body and a heavy heart,
Now straightway, if I think of it, become
Light as that bird wandering beyond my shore.

                            Edward Thomas

Of Mere Being

The palm at the end of the mind,
Beyond the last thought, rises
In the bronze distance.

A gold-feathered bird
Sings in the palm, without human meaning,
Without human feeling, a foreign song.

You know then that it is not the reason
That makes us happy or unhappy.
The bird sings. Its feathers shine.

The palm stands on the edge of space.
The wind moves slowly in the branches.
The bird's fire-fangled feathers dangle down.

                                        Wallace Stevens

The Tree in the Wood

There was a tree grew in the wood
The findest tree that ever was seen
The tree grew in the wood
The limb grew on the tree
A branch grew on the limb
A nest was on the branch
An egg was in the nest
A yolk was in the egg
A bird was in the yolk
A wing was on the bird
A feather was on the wing

And the green leaves growed all around around
  around
And the green leaves growed all around.

Anonymous

'"Hope" is the thing with feathers'

'Hope' is the thing with feathers –
That perches in the soul –
And sings the tune without the words –
And never stops – at all –

And sweetest – in the Gale – is heard –
And sore must be the storm –
That could abash the little Bird
That kept so many warm –

I've heard it in the chillest land –
And on the strangest Sea –
Yet, never, in Extremity,
It asked a crumb – of Me.

Emily Dickinson

Afterword

Despite recent attempts to make it a hands-on, interactive experience, Huddersfield's Tolson Museum retains a traditional atmosphere, full of old costumes and excavated pots. The recommended route through the building will lead the visitor towards a recreated Victorian classroom, past some early examples of the motor car, up the stairs and along a corridor leading smartly from the Palaeolithic Age to the Industrial Revolution, before culminating in the infamous Bird Room, a room so unforgettable it forms part of the town's collective consciousness. As a child I was both disturbed and fascinated by the Bird Room. Inside, glass cabinets are stacked wall-to-wall and floor-to-ceiling. Within each cabinet is a stuffed bird, configured so as to display some aspect of its behaviour, and set against a painted background depicting its natural habitat. So the scheming cuckoo is caught in the act of depositing its egg in another bird's nest. And the mischievous jackdaw is about to disappear down a chimney, possibly to build a nest, possibly to steal the princess's shiny gold ring. The Hitchcockian centre-piece of the collection is a golden eagle tearing off the flesh of an unfortunate rabbit.

Time has not been kind to the exhibited birds. Most of the specimens appear shrunken or withered, and sunlight has bleached the sheen and colour from the feathers of most, with the exception of the flamboyant peacock. The pair of hoopoes are looking particularly crest-fallen and monochromatic. Surprisingly, many of the birds were caught in the Huddersfield area, including several species that would be considered rare and exotic today. But without any acknowledgement of irony, the captions beneath some of the cases, such as that of the eagle owl and the Montagu's harrier, seem to imply that the bird behind the glass and the last local sighting of the said species are one and the same. On many levels the exhibition is a horror show, and even the man who presided over the shooting and stuffing, the teetotal and eventually devout Seth Lister Mosley, came to regret his years of 'murder and plunder'. Yet there remains something magical and alluring about the Bird Room, something inspiring and compelling about the bewildering range of birds and their beguiling names.

My father wasn't a bird-watcher but he knew what he was looking at when he saw one, and he fed them in the winter, scattering bread crumbs on the lawn or hanging gobbets of lard from the bird table in the garden. In my memory, the view of the village from the picture-window in my parents' front room is forever foregrounded by blue tits and coal tits on the feeder, and a magpie in its killer whale livery waiting menacingly in the lilac tree. On more than one occasion we drove to Bempton on Yorkshire's east coast, so as to crawl on all fours towards the cliff edge and peer downwards on a scene that looked like the ornithological re-enactment of the Battle of Britain, with untold varieties of sea-birds crowding the air-space and gannets dive-bombing the water. I started bird-watching when I stopped star-gazing, trading a telescope for a pair of binoculars. Staring into the heavens was all well and good for a poet, but in the end, stars refuse to be little more than small points of light – old light at that – whose relevance to life on earth is largely mathematical. I swapped stars for birds, far livelier performers and creatures whose working hours coincided more conveniently with my own, i.e. daylight. Like my father, my bird-watching doesn't extend much beyond wanting to recognize something when it enters my field of vision, although I care enough about birds to be a card-carrying member of the million-strong RSPB, and I write poems about them as well.

The difficulty in assembling this anthology of bird poetry was not deciding what to include but what to leave out. The book could have been three or four times its current size and would still have been nothing like an exhaustive or definitive survey. A glance through our index is enough to demonstrate that poets have written about birds from the very beginning; *why* they have done so is another matter, and probably a matter for speculation rather than certainty. One reason, as Tim Dee has suggested elsewhere, is their apparentness. Birds are, for most people, the most frequently seen of all creatures, and it would be virtually impossible to spend a day on Earth without seeing or hearing a bird, no matter what corner of the planet. But the relationship between poetry and birds is more than a function of familiarity. Poets, I believe, seek and find in the world of birds unlimited and unequalled reflections of their own world. In their extinctions and predicaments they are icons of environmentalism; in their colours and costumes they are a huge cast of characters; through the opportunity to list and catalogue them they speak to our obsessions and compulsions; with their talons and beaks they excite our phobias and fears; in their habits and behaviour they mirror certain human tendencies; in their mythologies and lore they are libraries of narrative and parable; in their shapes and silhouettes they are hieroglyphic alphabets. And so on. Perhaps at some subconscious, secular level they are also our souls. Or more likely, they are our poems. What we find in them we would hope for our work – that sense of soaring otherness. Maybe that's how poets think of birds: as poems.

Of all the poets gathered here, two deserve particular mention. John Clare wrote during the great period of nature writing, and lived closer to nature than most of the other Romantic poets put together, so we shouldn't be surprised that he wrote about birds. What *is* surprising is the extent of his bird poetry, and the accuracy of his observations. Through poetic ornithology he expressed not just his relationship to nature but, both directly and indirectly, his political convictions and personal sensibilities. John Clare is *the* bird poet – his bird poems are his best, and are the indispensable keystone to the construction of this book. About a hundred years after Clare's death, Ted Hughes was busily re-presenting the case for nature writing when most other poets of his generation were focused on urban or sociological themes. As someone who used language to make poetic and shamanistic flights of fancy, birds were pivotal to Hughes's approach. Those who have appreciated the living force of his poetry – many of them for the first time as schoolchildren – will have experienced a kind of magic, in which birds are not simply witnessed but brought to life, or brought *into* life on the page.

The poet Christopher Reid once compared the act of anthologizing with that of populating the ark, suggesting that Noah was our first ever anthologist. In this project, my role has been that of co-curator, designing and assembling a new Bird Room in which the captured birds are encased by nothing more than words.

Simon Armitage

Notes

These are intended to give a little background information on the specific birds mentioned in the poems. Whole books could be written on almost any of the species and some have been; the notes here are selective and subjective.

Ostrich

He 'Digesteth Harde Yron' – Marianne Moore

Marianne Moore's title comes from John Lyly who said (in his *Euphues*, 1579) the ostrich ate hard iron to preserve its health. In Shakespeare's *Henry VI, Part II* Jack Cade threatens Sir Alexander Iden: 'I'll make thee eat iron like an ostrich.' The ostrich is listed in the Old Testament as unclean and not to be eaten – it was banned probably because it mixes the odd lizard or snake into its otherwise vegetarian diet; perhaps also because – like a whale – it is a creature somehow out of place, a bird that is not quite a bird. Its scientific name (as Marianne Moore notes) means the camel-bird. A Persian proverb: 'They said to the camel-bird, "Take up a load"; he replied, "I am a bird." They said, "Fly"; he said, "I am a camel."' They are famous for their unscrupulous snacking: barbed wire and bullets have been found in their stomachs, fifty-three diamonds in one bird, an alarm clock, three gloves and some small change in another. The ostrich is the largest living bird and just about counts as European – it features in the monumental *Birds of the Western Palearctic* (on the basis of a tiny nomadic population in the western Sahara) but it has also long strayed (leggily and monumentally) into the European mind. North African Neolithic rock art includes an archer aiming at an ostrich. In the mid-1600s Sir Thomas Browne and his son Edward kept ostriches in Norfolk: 'Whosoever shall compare and consider together the ostrich and the tomineio, or humbird, not weighing twelve grains, may easily discover under what compass or latitude the creation of birds has been ordained.' Later both Coleridge and Wordsworth imported metaphorical ostriches into their autobiographies. Coleridge: 'I have laid too many eggs in the hot sands of this wilderness, the world, with ostrich carelessness and ostrich oblivion.' Wordsworth: 'Thence, forth I ran/ From that assembly, through a length of streets/Ran ostrich-like to reach our chapel door . . .' Ostriches do not bury their heads in sand. Threatened birds, though more likely to retaliate with ninja kicks and savage bites, do sometimes hide by lying down, stretching their neck and head along the ground. Three gathered white billowing ostrich feathers have formed the crest of the Prince of Wales for more than six hundred years; the same three are on the tails side of a two pence piece. There was an ostrich boom in Britain in the early 1990s when up to 20,000 birds were farmed. But the bubble burst and numbers are now considerably lower. Meanwhile the flesh is rich and dark like red meat and the Standing Committee of the European Convention for the Protection of Animals Kept for Farming Purposes runs a detailed website on its recommendations concerning optimum rearing conditions for ratites (ostriches, emus and rheas).

Marianne Moore's poem mentions solitaires. They were close relatives to dodos, lived on Rodrigues and were hunted to extinction in the mid-1700s.

Emperor Penguin

On the Death of an Emperor Penguin in Regent's Park – David Wright

Penguins, whatever David Wright says in his poem, are not closely related to auks. They live like flightless auks but their evolutionary paths have converged towards one another rather than diverged from the same source. The emperor is the tallest and heaviest of all penguins. Its dives can last up to twenty minutes and go as deep as 1,800 feet. It breeds during the Antarctic winter and treks, through horrendous conditions, up to seventy-five miles to and from its breeding rookeries. There are no longer any emperor penguins at London Zoo. The famous penguin pool – like a sliced hard-boiled egg – designed in 1934 by Bertold Lubetkin, is now home to rockhopper and black-footed (or jackass) penguins.

Albatross

The Albatross – Charles Baudelaire (translated by Richard Wilbur)
from The Rime of the Ancient Mariner – Samuel Taylor Coleridge

There are twenty-one albatross species in the world; they only occur in European waters as vagrants. All are pelagic birds with colossal wingspans (up to eleven feet), able to glide over oceans for miles and hours on end, but comically inept (as Baudelaire says, 'he cannot walk') at landing and taking off. Most summers between 1972 and 1995 a black-browed albatross dubbed – inevitably – 'Albert Ross' joined the breeding gannets on the offshore stacks and cliffs at Hermaness on Unst in Shetland, the most northerly point of Britain. It had no luck. The species is declining very rapidly at its breeding colonies in the South Atlantic (80 per cent breed on the Falkland Islands – and so are a British responsibility if not exactly a British bird) and is considered endangered. The decline is attributed to the birds accidentally getting entangled with fishing long-lines and trawl nets. Wordsworth claimed that he had given Coleridge the idea of an albatross for his 'Rime of the Ancient Mariner' having read of the birds being sighted around Cape Horn. The first accepted British record dates from 1897 – 101 years after Coleridge figured his.

Gannet

Rhu Mor – Norman MacCaig
Candlebird – Don Paterson

At any daytime moment, somewhere around Britain's shores, a gannet will be folding itself up to become a brilliant white arrowhead slicing into the sea below it after fish (to 'explode the green into white', as Norman MacCaig says). Two hundred and twenty thousand pairs breed on British cliffs and offshore islands. The gannet and people go back a long way. Gannet bones have been found added to the mounds of heaped shell fragments of Oronsay off the west coast of Scotland. These middens – the earliest record of human-avian entanglement in Britain – are 6,000 years old. One of the latest updates to the story is Ian Dury's song 'Billericay Dickie' where he rhymes 'Isle of Thanet' with 'Janet', 'prannet', 'plan it' and 'gannet' (as in 'she looked more like a gannet'). Licensed guga hunting – young gannets are called gugas in the Hebrides – by a boat load of Hebridean men continues to this day. When St Kilda was inhabited, its population lived from its breeding gannets, fulmars and puffins, which were taken for food, feathers and oil. The seabirds' fish-oil rich diet made them ignitable as 'candlebirds', as Don Paterson's poem details. J. H. Gurney wrote the biography of the gannet in 1913 – one of the first ever monographs of a bird. Its name, he says, comes from the 'Scottish language' where to gant or gaunt means to yawn by opening the mouth. Gurney translated early accounts of the bird including this description by Robert Gordon (published in Latin in 1654) of the birds on the Bass Rock at the mouth of the Firth of Forth where to this day they swirl in their thousands around the great crowned head of volcanic phonolite:

This island has . . . a quite wonderful bird called the Bass Goose, somewhat smaller than a Common Goose, but much fatter, for they live on Herrings, and have the same taste when eaten. They surpass in fatness all other birds, of whatever kind they be . . . They have a long neck like the Crane's, and a very sharp beak, as long as our longest finger, and yellow in colour. The bone which we commonly call 'the bril' [the furcula] in other birds can be separated from the breast-bone, but in these Geese it cannot; indeed so firm is it that no force can divide it, and it is attached in this manner to the breast-bone in order that when they chase the Herrings, and plunge into the sea, they should not break their necks by their extreme violence . . . Many of them, nevertheless, are killed in the following manner. The sailors prepare a smooth board, and make it white, and fasten herrings on it; which board they make fast to the stern of a fishing boat. The Geese, seeing the Herrings, try to seize them with their beak, and drive it so deep into the board that they cannot pull it out again, and thus are taken, or rather take themselves.

Blue Booby

The Blue Booby – James Tate

This is better known as a blue-footed booby, *Sula nebouxii*. Boobies are close relatives of gannets. Their name comes from the Spanish 'bobo' meaning stupid or fool or clown. It describes their clumsiness on land, their tameness and their slightly cross-eyed dorkish expression. The blue-footed booby nests along the eastern edge of the Pacific Ocean from the Galapagos archipelago to California. The bird's blue feet – a clean salted blue like the blue of the Greek flag – are important during courtship displays when the male performs a high-stepping dance. The bluer the feet the more attractive the male.

James Tate suggests the birds gather blue objects, like bowerbirds, as part of their courtship. They don't.

Cormorant

The Common Cormorant – Christopher Isherwood
To be Engraved on the Skull of a Cormorant – Charles Tomlinson

The cormorant and the shag look superficially similar but are two different species. The shag is a more marine bird with an iridescent green-black plumage. Cormorants have various white patches and more of a black-suited sheen about them. They look old where shags look reptilian. The oldest cormorant recorded in Britain lived for twenty-three years. There are about 8,500 pairs. Cormorants' feathers are not waterproof although they spend their lives in the water – this is why we see them hanging themselves out to dry with their outstretched wings after they have been fishing. A beautiful painting (dated to the early 1490s) in the Getty Museum in Los Angeles by Vittore Carpaccio shows fishermen using cormorants to fish for them in the Venice lagoon in a kind of underwater falconry. In China and Japan the use of cormorants as living harpoons has continued at least until recent times – the birds being made to wear a leather collar to prevent them eating the fish they catch. The bird is traditionally thought to be greedy – the sight of them dealing with a fish taken on a dive, tossing and positioning their catch so it can be better swallowed, perhaps contributes to this impression. All of Shakespeare's mentions of the bird reflect this – a man's 'cormorant belly' in *Coriolanus*, 'cormorant devouring time' in *Love's Labour's Lost*, 'this cormorant war' in *Troilus and Cressida*. Coleridge told his brother that for three years he read for at least eight hours a day and described himself as a 'library-cormorant'. Milton describes Satan, 'this first grand thief into God's fold', flying into the Tree of Life where he 'sat like a cormorant . . . devising Death'.

Grey Heron

The Heron – Paul Farley
Heron – Helen Dunmore

There are more than 600 heronries in Britain. Every summer they contain 14,000 twiggy nests. A census of heronries has been underway since 1928 and is the longest-running breeding-season bird-monitoring scheme in the world. It shows the species to be more abundant than it has ever been before. Being great eel hunters, grey herons have been watched and emulated. Pieces of the bird's legs have been scattered in the water as magic bait, other human fishermen carried a heron's foot in their pocket as a talisman. When Hamlet declares his sanity by saying that he knows a 'hawk from a handsaw' (2.ii.272), he means he knows the difference between a hawk and heron. Handsaw is a contracted, rubbed with use, version of 'heronshaw', an old name for the heron. Hawks were flown at herons (Richard Lovelace's poem 'The Falcon' describes this) and herons were eaten. On 22 and 23 September 1465 at a feast for a new archbishop of York, 400 herons were called for (along with 2,000 geese, 500 stags, 608 pike and bream and 12 porpoises and seals).

Mute Swan

Leda and the Swan – W. B. Yeats

Zeus came to Leda in the form of a swan and raped her. Four children (two by Zeus, two by her husband) hatched from eggs. How she laid them is not known. Lost paintings by both Leonardo da Vinci and Michelangelo showed how the artists imagined a swan having sex with a woman. The Michelangelo (a sixteenth-century copy is in the National Gallery in London) is particularly graphic: Leda's muscular left leg and the swan's extended right wing are entwined, the swan's tail pushes down between Leda's legs, just as it does when the birds keep their sex to themselves.

The feathery creak of swans' wings in flight, like stretched sail-cloth in the wind, makes one of the most striking and beautiful of bird noises.

But can a swan's wing break a man's arm? Gulliver is 'boxed' by a Brobdingnagian 'Linnet somewhat larger than an English Swan'. Mute swans are among the heaviest flying birds in the world but still weigh far less than an adult human. The website of the Swan Sanctuary of Shepperton (whose facilities include an intensive care ward and a re-habilitation lake) reports that it is 'theoretically possible' if a wing 'in full span and velocity were to hit a weak-boned person'. The Sanctuary also reports that 'as a general rule' it is true that swans mate for life and those that are widowed 'go through a grieving process'. Do swans sing only before they die (Tennyson's 'death-hymn')? No, despite its common name, the mute swan is not silent. It has a repertoire of hisses and grunts. But so-called 'wild' swans (see below) are far more musical.

Whooper Swan

The Wild Swans at Coole – W. B. Yeats
Postscript – Seamus Heaney

There are two 'wild' swan species – the whooper (named for its call) and Bewick's (named for the engraver). Both breed in high latitudes across northern Europe and winter to the south. The mute swan – now living freely throughout Britain and Ireland – is commonly thought to have been introduced by the Romans or by Richard I, but bones of mute swans have been found in Pleistocene peat deposits suggesting the birds have been in Britain for much longer. However, the mute swan's association with royalty (there are said to be 900 ways of marking a swan's beak to indicate its owner) and its year-round presence on ponds and lakes in towns and city parks have sustained the idea that the birds are somehow not totally wild. The marvellous polar white of whooper swans, their black and buttercup bills and their Arctic bugling calls across a wind-lashed lough on the Irish Atlantic coast belong to an altogether different swan experience. Ireland is a wintering stronghold for the species and it is no accident that it features so prominently as an Irish poetical bird. The Finnish composer Einojuhani Rautavaara has woven the calls of whooper swans alongside a symphony orchestra to great effect in his 'Cantus Arcticus' (1972).

Goose

Ancient Egyptians domesticated geese. European farmyard geese are derived from greylags, the wild goose that today seems on the point of giving up being wild. Greylags in Britain are a mixture of more or less wild birds (those that breed in Iceland come for the winter) and more or less tame or feral geese. They have set up shop alongside introduced Canada geese and a motley array of other half-farm half-wild birds. Nothing shows our botched tenancy of the planet quite like a mixed flight of geese (Canadas, greylags, maybe a snow goose or a Muscovy duck) above a motorway in southern England moving from one gravel pit to another. An entry in Coleridge's notebook reads: '[a] Goose would be a noble Bird if it did not remind us of the Swan'.

Pliny the Elder reports how honking geese saved the Roman Capitol from night attacks by Gauls in 390 BC. Manlius the ex-consul was woken by geese cackling in the Temple of Juno and so was able to save the city. The event was marked each year 'by paying honour to the descendants of the sacred geese, whose cries gave warning of the enemy's approach, adorning them with jewels and carrying them about in litters, but also by crucifying a dog, as a punishment for the want of vigilance shown by its progenitors on that occasion'.

Wild greylags breed in Scotland and several other geese species winter there. Kathleen Jamie's are unidentified but her description of their 'lowin'' calls like cattle suggests they are pink-footed geese. White-fronted geese laugh, greylags honk and barnacle geese yap.

Wigeon

Can be spelled with a 'd' or without. Four hundred thousand birds winter in Britain and around 500 pairs breed; large numbers winter in Ireland too. Wigeon like to graze, and winter bird-watching trips to freezing reservoirs or dreary estuaries are often brightened by flocks of the ducks cropping at the grass and whistling as they go. Their call is shivery but companionable.

Mandarin Duck

Mandarin Duck – Richard Price

The drake mandarin in breeding plumage is a baffling mixture of oranges and browns and golds with flaming whiskers and sail-shaped extensions to its back feathers. It looks overdesigned. It swims but seems to be doing a fan dance. Mandarins are native to China but were introduced to Britain sometime before the mid-eighteenth century and there are now 7,000 birds scattered across central and southern England. They nest in holes in trees.

Eagle

The Dalliance of the Eagles – Walt Whitman

Eagles, like hawks and falcons, occur repeatedly in poetry and are used by poets as totemic birds with even less specificity. There are two widespread eagles in North America that Whitman might have seen, the bald and the golden. We cannot be sure and, to complicate things, some hawks are called eagles and some eagles are called hawks. What is certain from Whitman's poem is the sense that he actually saw what he wrote about – the two birds grappling in mid-air and tumbling earthwards. He attributes this to a male and female in display. The rugged ballet could just as easily have been rival birds clashing over territory.

Red Kite

Red Kites at Tregaron – Gwyneth Lewis

Tregaron – in mid-Wales – where Gwyneth Lewis's poem is set was until the last few years the most reliable place, especially in winter, to see red kites in Britain. The species, once widespread and common, had been persecuted so effectively by gamekeepers and hunters to the point, through most of the twentieth century, that its only refuge was the high sheep-walks, the wind-hammered hill tops and a few green oak valleys between them around Tregaron. Protection for the bird and a concerted and highly successful campaign of reintroduction has changed all this. Gorgeous flotillas of kites, like straying sheets of beaten copper, can now be seen busking above the back gardens of Didcot or managing their own traffic over the M40 near High Wycombe. The time may not be so far off, once again, where a visiting ambassador (as happened in London in the winter of 1496) might report kites in the city, 'so tame, that they often take out of the hands of little children, the bread smeared with butter . . . given to them by their mothers'.

Secretary Bird

Secretary Bird – Alan Ross

Secretary birds are good candidates for a dinosaur-bird. They look ancient and composite, half-raptor half-stork, long-legged and hook-beaked. They live on African grasslands and though they can fly they hunt their food on foot, striding like veteran power walkers through the savannah. They eat insects, small mammals, birds and their eggs. They grab their prey with their beaks or stamp on it with their powerful feet. The bird's English name comes from the writing-quill-like feathers that extend from the bird's crown and neck.

Hawk and Falcon

The Hawk – George Mackay Brown
Hawk Roosting – Ted Hughes
Tamer and Hawk – Thom Gunn

Poets are drawn to raptors. Though both poems by Ted Hughes and Thom Gunn cite hawks, it seems more likely that the poets actually refer to falcons. The hawks of Ted Hughes's world would have been sparrowhawks, which hunt by stealth, exploiting cover and surprise rather than supremacy of flight. Thom Gunn's hawk hovers, he says, which hawks do not but falcons do (kestrels above all – see 'The Windhover'). George Mackay Brown's hawk might be a sparrowhawk or a buzzard or is perhaps just a compound bird of prey. Hen harriers are a speciality of Orkney where Mackay Brown lived and wrote, but the hunting bird described in his poem does not do what harriers do. A recording of the poet reading the poem is available at *www.poetryarchive.org*.

Kestrel

The Windhover – Gerard Manley Hopkins

With Hopkins's poem we are in no doubt as to the species he is describing. The windhover is an old name for a kestrel, but even without this aid, his annotation of a bird of prey hovering is a very accurate description. Even hard-to-impress and unpoetical county bird recorders would surely accept Hopkins's record.

Around 1600 both Thomas Nashe and Ben Jonson used another, even more visually demonstrative term for a kestrel when they called it a 'wind fucker', Nashe writing of 'kistrilles or windfuckers that filling themselves with winde, fly against the winde evermore'.

Turkey

Turkey-Cock – D. H. Lawrence

Turkeys are native to North America and Mexico. They were domesticated there long before Europeans arrived. At Cobá in Mexico, a Mayan city, there is evidence of domesticated birds from 100 BC. Native peoples across North America ate turkey meat and eggs and used the bird's feathers for decorative objects and clothing and its bones for musical instruments and tools. Spanish colonists took turkeys back to Europe; descendants of these birds were in turn taken back to America by later generations of colonists.

Why the turkey is called the turkey has been much debated. Christopher Leahy:

Gruson says that it is a Tartar word (meaning 'brave') used in the sixteenth century to refer both to Asia Minor but also very generally, to any form of exotica. There is some evidence that guinea fowls were the original avian 'turkeys' so named because they were imported from Africa to Europe via Turkey or simply because of the connection with Ottoman exoticism. When an even more bizarre fowl arrived in Europe from America, it captured the misnomer. In Turkey on the other hand turkeys are called Hindi, implying (incorrectly of course) that they came from another exotic place – India.

The turkey arrived in Britain around 1530 and in little more than a decade was 'bred so successfully that Archbishop Cranmer had to forbid his clergy to serve more than one turkey at a banquet'.

Cock and Hen

On a Cock at Rochester – Sir Charles Sedley
Cock-Crow – Edward Thomas
To a Prize Bird – Marianne Moore
Cock-Crows – Ted Hughes
The Chicken without a Head – Charles Simic

Most chickens are descendants of the red jungle fowl of Asia. Some sort of chicken has been kept by man for thousands of years. In India jungle fowl may have been domesticated before 3000 BC. In China they were being bred by 1400 BC, when they were described as 'the domesticated animal that knows the time'. Despite the crowing cockerel's part in the betrayal of Christ, there are few chickens in the Old Testament of the Bible: 'Birds among the Hebrews were a very unimportant item in domestic economy. They were rarely domesticated; indeed before the return from Babylon, it does not appear that any domestic poultry were ordinarily reared.' In September 1945, Mike, a rooster on a farm in Colorado, had his head cut off, ready for the pot. He lived on decapitated – the axe had missed his carotid artery and most of his brain stem was intact – for a further eighteen months. He was authenticated by the University of Utah, featured in *Time* and *Life* magazines, toured side-shows and earned his farmer owner $4,500 a month.

Capercaillie

Capercaillies – Paul Muldoon

The capercaillie is a giant forest grouse. They live in old pinewoods. Formerly found in northern England, Ireland and Scotland, in Britain they are now confined to a few ancient stretches of woodland in the Highlands of Scotland. They became extinct there in the 1770s and were reintroduced in the 1830s to Perthshire. Latest surveys suggest a maximum of 2,758 individuals. In spring their leks or communal displays are extraordinary spectacles of boreal theatre. At dawn, males – heavy glossy-black birds with their tails raised behind them like black half moons – gather together, dance, duel and sing the weirdest of love songs for the more retiring and smaller, brown-and-grey barred females who look on at the show. The song includes belching, bellowing and an imitation of corks popping, all accelerating into a great harrumph of feathers.

Pheasant

Pheasant – Sylvia Plath

To many British bird-watchers pheasants barely count as birds. It is certainly hard to claim them as wild. If the Romans didn't introduce them, as was long believed, then the Normans in the eleventh century certainly did. And to this day 20 million are raised and released every year in Britain for shooting. Close on half of these are shot in their first season. Pheasants are little studied by bird-watchers; one note in the journal *British Birds* described a hen pheasant successfully swimming on the sea in Scotland in 1952 and ended: 'This is probably the only known case of a pheasant doing something interesting.' If they were rare though, the cock pheasant's plumage would excite great wonder, with its long fanciful tail, red facial wattles like saucers of blood, iridescent green-black head, and richly spotted brown back that suggests it is wearing a mantle of pearls.

Corncrake

The Corn Craiks Rispy Song – John Clare
The Landrail – John Clare
First Corncrake – John Hewitt
Corncrakes – Louis MacNeice
A Voice of Summer – Norman MacCaig

The corncrake, a streaky grass-coloured crake living in fields of streaky grass, is now a rarity in Britain, except on a few islands in the Hebrides. About 1,000 males have been counted singing in recent years. In Ireland it is also much reduced and survives only in the Shannon Callows, north Donegal and western parts of Mayo and Connaught. Corncrakes are heard far more than seen, they are very secretive birds and reluctant fliers and it is hard to conceive of their migration each winter to the grasslands of sub-Saharan Africa. The bird (also known as a landrail) was once widespread throughout Britain and Ireland and the male's call, perfectly described by the bird's Latin name, *Crex crex*, was the rasping sound of summer nights in almost all grassed areas. Loss of hay meadows, the conversion of hay to silage and the early cutting of hay all contributed to the bird's demise. They survive now where difficult terrain makes mechanized mowing hard and where late haymaking still takes place. Major conservation initiatives in Britain and Ireland are underway and in the fenland washes of eastern England a reintroduction scheme is showing first signs of success.

Lapwing

Two Pewits – Edward Thomas
Plovers – Paul Muldoon

Lapwings are still widely known as pewits (also spelled peewit), after their commonly recognized call. Their beautiful flopping flight over bare fields, as if they are dabbing at the wet spring sky, is still a feature of the British countryside though the birds have faced a catastrophic decline in numbers. Changes in farming practices have prompted an 80 per cent decline in lapwing numbers in Britain since 1960.

The lapwing is a plover and Paul Muldoon's poem could be about them but it also suggests another bird, a golden plover, whose Latin family name *Pluvialis* means rain and whose flights are characterized by somewhat sudden and startled arrivals and departures – just as rain can start up and stop in a squally fashion.

Sandpiper

Sandpiper – Elizabeth Bishop

Identifying Elizabeth Bishop's sandpiper is hard, though the poem is made out of plenty of real looking. Nearly ninety species of birds might be called sandpipers and many of these behave at the sea's edge as Bishop's birds do. Sanderlings are tiny waders common on both sides of the Atlantic. They run to the sea's edge and away from it on short black legs that whirr faster than the eye can see. But larger waders also commute along the sea's edge and feed there. American bird-watching has the lovely generic name 'peep' for small *Calidris* sandpipers, which captures their soft contact calls, but also describes their investigatory progress along the tide line.

Curlew

Curlew – Gillian Clarke

After the lapwing and the oystercatcher, the curlew is probably the best-known shorebird in Britain. It is the largest wader. Its name and its call seem to capture the bird's essence, evoking the open moors it breeds on, the mudflats it winters along, and even the curve of its beak and its rounded brown back. W. S. Graham has a line in a poem describing the curlew's call as a 'love weep'. At Jarlshof in southern Shetland, Iron Age curlew bones have been excavated, suggesting the bird was eaten then. Curlews still call as they fly over the remains of the settlement there. The curlew features in the Anglo-Saxon poem 'The Seafarer' as a *huilpe*, this in turn becomes the Scottish *whaup* and the Dutch *wulp* for curlew. In Welsh a curlew is *y gylfinir*.

A cantref is a Welsh term for a Welsh parcel of land – smaller than most counties, larger than most parishes.

Greenshank

Greenshank – Norman MacCaig

Norman MacCaig's poem describes greenshanks as breeding birds. About 1,500 pairs breed in the remote and boggy flow country of northern Scotland. They are rare and elegant birds – with long but fine washed-green legs and silvery lichen-coloured wings and backs, blending perfectly into the Scottish tundra. Most British bird-watchers are more familiar with the birds on passage, when greenshanks turn up on the edge of drying reservoirs or along estuaries on their way out of the country to their wintering grounds around the Mediterranean and south through the length of Africa. The birds are often first detected by their clear and ringing flight call: *chew chew chew*. They always sound nervous. They walk with a similar diligence.

Snipe

To the Snipe – John Clare
The Backward Look – Seamus Heaney

Snipe are, for most of the year, secretive and skulking, wonderfully camouflaged and hard to see on the ground and only rising, when flushed, in a great haste of escape. But when displaying in the spring, they bleat or drum, flying over their squelchy places, calling with a rhythmic tick-tocking *chip chip chip chip* and then scrambling up the sky to fall back towards the earth with their bills pointed down and their tails splayed with their outer feathers gapped which, as the birds dive, produce a whirring feathery drumming sound. They are hard to shoot – to 'snipe' and a 'sniper' has the bird's name at their root – but good to eat. The annual bag in Britain is still around 85,000. As wet places have been drained snipe have got more rare as breeding birds. In John Clare's time they were being captured for food in a marsh where the mansions of Belgravia now stand.

Kittiwake

At Marsden Bay – Peter Reading

The gentlest looking of all the gulls, the kittiwake's name comes from its call. Fishermen were believed to turn into gulls when they died while dead children became kittiwakes. They breed on sea cliffs and range over the whole of the North Atlantic. It is a true seagull. Probably because of the collapse of sand eel stocks, the British population is suffering catastrophically in some areas – with no young being fledged and adult numbers halved over the last twenty years. An urban colony – the furthest inland breeding site for the species in the world – nests on the metal gantry of the Tyne Bridge in Newcastle. When ladies wore feathers in their hats, the black and white zigzags on the wings of young kittiwakes were much sought. Seven hundred were killed in one day for this purpose on Lundy in Devon. Until the 1950s kittiwakes and their eggs were collected for food along the Yorkshire coast and elsewhere. In May 2001 a gunman shot and killed eighty kittiwakes at Marsden Bay in South Tyneside (scene of Peter Reading's earlier poem) and laid them out on the beach beneath the cliff there to spell 'Death'.

Dodo

Ye haue heard this yarn afore – Peter Reading

Eighty years after the Dutch discovered it on Mauritius in the early seventeenth century, the dodo – a relative of pigeons and doves – was extinct. They were flightless, confiding birds and laid their eggs on the ground. Oliver Goldsmith wrote: 'It is a silly simple bird . . . and very easily taken. Three or four dodos are enough to dine a hundred men.' Despite all the eating there are no complete dodo skeletons anywhere in the world. Stuffed dodos in museums are models. The Grant Museum of Zoology at University College, London has a box of twenty or so bones. It looks like a tub of chicken remains after a fast-food blowout. A part skeleton found recently in a cave in Mauritius may yet yield dodo DNA. It is the dodo in *Alice's Adventures in Wonderland* that engineers the race that ends when it says, 'Everybody has won and all must have prizes.'

Rock Dove/Feral Pigeon

'I had a dove and the sweet dove died' – John Keats
Pigeons – Marianne Moore
Pigeons – Philip Larkin
Pigeons at Dawn – Charles Simic

If the pheasant struggles to be loved by bird-watchers, the feral pigeon is beyond the pale. While it could be more legitimately added to a day-list than a chicken crossing the road, the grey town pigeon must be one of the most seen but most overlooked of birds. Yet pigeon fanciers – a human subspecies also ignored by bird-watchers though steeped in bird knowledge – love their birds. Pigeons have been domesticated and their homing skills exploited for thousands of years. Modern racing began in Belgium in the mid-nineteenth century. One reason birders are not keen is perhaps their sense of feral pigeons swamping their ancestor, the much rarer and more elusive rock dove that lives on cliffs and in caves and commonly far from man. Feral pigeons with their feet like meteorites – often managing with stumps instead of toes – and their well-attested ability to hop on to tube trains in London instead of flying across the city seem a little too close to home.

Rimbaud spent some time living in Reading not long before his exit from Europe and from poetry. While there he kept lists of English words he came across. One is of pigeons: 'homing, working, fantails, pearl-eyed tumbler, shortfaced, performing tumblers, trumpeters, squeakers, blue, red turbits, Jacobins, baldpates, pearl eyes, tumbles well, high flying performing tumblers, splashed, rough legged, grouse limbed, black buglers, saddle back, over thirty tail feathers'.

Wood Pigeon

Wood-Pigeons – Vicki Feaver

A panic-struck wood pigeon clattering away through the branches of a tree or a wing clapping bird on its display flight make two of the most familiar bird noises in Britain. Its song – asthmatic breathing through a quilt – is another, a feature of summer days when almost every other bird has stopped singing. The wood pigeon is one of the most numerous and widely distributed birds in the country. It is an agricultural pest – one bird's crop and stomach contained 1,020 grains of corn, another's 198 beans and another's 20 small potatoes. As a consequence it can be hunted year-round. As many as 8 million birds have been shot in one year. Its flesh is dark but delicate and flavoursome. Squabs are particularly tender. James Fenton in his selection of Coleridge's poems cites a fragment that gives a North Country or Borders dialect word for the wood pigeon: 'Or wren or linnet/In Bush and Bushet:/No tree but in it/A cooing cushat.' Fenton adds, 'This is what a poem looks like in the egg.'

Orange Dove

The Orange Dove of Fiji – James Fenton

This is *Ptilinopus victor*. Males are vivid fiery orange. They are confined to open forest in Fiji, but no longer thought threatened. They fly like thrown orange hand grenades, fast and direct with whirring wingbeats.

Emerald Dove

The Emerald Dove – Les Murray

Breeds from India south and east to northern Australia. It has a metallic green back and wings. It feeds on the ground, primarily on seeds and fallen fruits, and walks and runs nimbly. *Paua* is a Maori word for a large edible abalone; the shell is a richly coloured oily emerald green.

Collared Dove

Listening to Collared Doves – E. J. Scovell

The collared dove has become so commonplace, its call note and sandy flickering flight so embedded in suburb life, that it is now hard to imagine they didn't breed in Britain until 1955. The reasons for the expansion, north and west, are unknown. From their original home in India they had spread and had reached Turkey in the sixteenth century. But the middle years of the twentieth century was the collared dove's blitzkrieg. They first bred in Hungary in 1932, in Germany in 1945, in France in 1952 and in Cromer in Norfolk in 1955. In 2000 there were 284,000 collared dove territories in Britain. They have now reached Iceland.

Parrot

Parrot – Stevie Smith

There are 332 species of parrots world wide. Most warm and tropical regions have parrots and now many temperate zones do too. Escaped and introduced parrots are often highly successful colonists. The Carolina parakeet – a native North American parrot – became extinct at the beginning of the twentieth century but, a hundred years on, Los Angeles and many other cities are crowded with tropical newcomers: fast flying green flashes chattering over intersections. Spanish cities and parts of London are also increasingly parrot places.

In the Buddhist Avadanas from India the story is told of the election of the bird king. The owl wins, as it is vigilant at night, but the parrot objects, saying that the owl cannot keep awake in the day, and promotes itself to the throne. Parrots can mimic human speech but they also seem to be able to understand it. Alex, an African grey parrot, was even able to answer questions as complex as 'How many red squares?' with over 80 per cent accuracy. A homemade film of a pet sulphur-crested cockatoo called Snowball dancing to rock music (viewable on YouTube) has recently been scientifically scrutinized and the bird's rhythmic stomps annotated. Snowball was able to keep time as the beat changed. Previously only humans were thought to have the ability to dance.

Parakeet

Bird Lady – Peter Reading

Parakeets, like the larger parrots, have a fast flight and garish calls. It is easy to imagine them crossing miles of tropical canopy like broken off patches of the lush green forest, heckling the woods as they go. Nowadays they are just as likely to be seen over the roofs of west London. Peter Reading's poem is set in Amsterdam, but the same species, the ring-necked parakeet, found in the wild in central Africa and southern Asia, is now naturalized and established in Britain, where 4,300 adults live around London, having first bred in Kent in 1969. They are hardy birds and often start nesting right at the beginning of the year. The population is growing and the species has been recorded in almost every English county and is now taking on Wales and Scotland. One account of the bird in Britain ends: 'Their penchant for fruit should signal a clear warning to fruit-growers and gardeners.'

Cuckoo

Cuckoo – Anonymous
The Cuckoo – Anonymous
To the Cuckoo – William Wordsworth
'Repeat that, repeat' – Gerard Manley Hopkins
Short Ode to the Cuckoo – W. H. Auden

The cuckoo's song, the sonic touchstone of spring – its 'two fold shout' as Wordsworth calls it – is heard less and less in Britain. The species is in decline, perhaps because its hosts – meadow pipits and dunnocks – are as well, perhaps because the caterpillars it eats are also depleted. One hundred years ago they were widespread across Britain except for Orkney and Shetland. Now they are uncommon.

Flickering black and white film survives from 1921. A female cuckoo – all long grey wings and tail – comes flying across the open scrub of Pound Green Common in Worcestershire and lands just in front of the camera. Meadow pipits leap up around the cuckoo, diving at its back to attack it, as if they know exactly what is happening. The unperturbed cuckoo crouches at their nest for a few seconds, lays her egg with her back to the camera then lifts and flies off. This film and the detailed fieldwork it captured of Edgar Chance, a West Midlands businessman and cuckoo obsessive, untangled some of the cuckoo's secrets for the first time. It was now proved that the cuckoo laid its egg directly in its host bird's nest. Cuckoo studies continue but the bird is so reduced in Britain that research projects – including the most important one at

Wicken Fen outside Cambridge – are now finding it hard to have enough cuckoos to watch.

The Times often published letters detailing the first cuckoos heard each spring in Britain: 'One year, the record was exceptionally early (in February), which two days later produced a highly sceptical reply from an eminent ornithologist, giving several reasons why the record was suspect. Two days later the same ornithologist received a parcel by post. It was the body of the cuckoo.'

Tawny Owl

'Sweet Suffolk owl' – Anonymous

The tawny owl is the 'to whit to whoo' owl. But this sound is probably two birds calling to each other. Male birds hoot or *whoo* and females have a more pointed *kewick* call. Gilbert White wrote: 'A neighbour of mine, who is said to have a nice ear, remarks that the owls about this village hoot in three different keys, in G flat, or F sharp, in B flat and A flat.' Tawny owls live in deciduous woodland. They are the most nocturnal British owl. There were 19,000 pairs in Britain in 2000.

Barn Owl

Barn Owl – R. S. Thomas

'A boy went in to a graveyard and shot a white owl. Then, seized with alarm, he rushed home in the greatest excitement screaming, "I've shot a cherubim".' Barn owls hunt over open country, often in the daytime as well as at night. There were a maximum of 5,000 pairs in Britain in 1997. Though declining in Britain, the barn owl is the most widely distributed land bird in the world, occurring throughout South America, Australia, most of Africa and the more temperate zones of the northern hemisphere.

Nightjar

The Fern Owls Nest – John Clare
The Dor-Hawk – Mary Howitt

Nightjars look like giant thin-winged moths. They live on heaths and hunt at night – eating the things they look like. Males on their breeding grounds *churr* a remarkable furry purr. They were long called (in several languages, including their Latin name) goat-suckers or goat-milkers and were believed to do just that. They probably acquired this name from being seen near livestock but their weirdness alone – a nocturnal vibrating half-moth half-owl – would be enough to prompt dark imaginings. Gilbert White recorded how nightjars were also believed to attack cattle with their beaks, infecting them with a disease called 'puckeridge', but noted that 'they are perfectly harmless, and subsist alone, being night birds, on night-insects'. The European summer population of nightjars (3,400 pairs breed in Britain) winters in Africa.

Whippoorwill

In Midsummer Quiet – Charles Simic

Henry Thoreau wrote in *Walden*: 'Regularly at half past seven, in one part of summer, after the evening train had gone by, the whippoorwills chanted their vespers for half an hour.' A North American nightjar, the bird's name comes from its song: a loud and carrying trio of notes with the accent on the first and the third and a weird theremin-like tremble in between, perfect for suggesting night time spookery. Hank Williams's brilliantly miserable song 'I'm So Lonesome I Could Cry' (written in 1949 and much covered since) begins: 'Hear the lonesome whippoor-will/He sounds too blue to fly.' The bird and the song seem to have evolved towards one another. Breeding whippoorwills synchronize their egg laying to lunar phases so chicks hatch on average ten days before a full moon, allowing the parent birds to feed through the whole moonlit night and so maximize their harvest of insects for their growing young.

Swift

The Swifts – Edward Thomas
Swifts – Ted Hughes

Swifts are one of the most apparently miraculous of familiar British birds. Though to call them British is not really accurate. The birds come here for no more than four months of the year and while they are here – though forced to nest and lay eggs and rear young – they touch the surface of the country as little as they possibly can. Their legs are short, their feet cling far better than they can walk, they prefer to fly straight into their nesting crannies in buildings, and drop back out of them into their real habitat, the air, where they are far more at home. They feed there, mate there (Gilbert White, 24 May 1785: 'Swifts copulate in the air, as they flie') and even sleep there. In August they vanish from above Britain, and fly non-stop to southern Africa where they spend eight months or more flying, non-stop once again.

Hummingbird

Humming-Bird – D. H. Lawrence

There are 328 species of hummingbird; they are among the world's weirdest birds. They occur only in the New World, but reach from Tierra del Fuego to southern Alaska. All are small, some are tiny – the smallest bird in the world is a bee hummingbird, endemic to Cuba – most are brilliantly coloured and zip with iridescent wildfire across our view, all fly with extraordinary speed (eighty wing beats a second) and manoeuvrability, and hover similarly, they feed on plant nectar and insects, and they call with electric buzzes and squeaks (their name comes from the audible whirr of their wings not their calls). Hummingbirds probably have the highest metabolism of any warm-blooded vertebrate (shrews might compete). They need to keep eating to stay alive. After days of bad or cold weather or when food has been scarce they have the ability to become torpid to survive the night. Their English names register the brilliance of the birds and some of our bafflement: hairy hermit, violet sabrewing, black Jacobin, sparkling violet-ear, green mango, fiery-tailed awlbill, crimson topaz, plovercrest, peacock coquette, snow-cap, purple-crowned woodnymph, empress brilliant, shining sunbeam, gorgeted sunangel, glowing puffleg, bearded mountaineer and so on. The list is like a logbook of fairies. Alexander Pope is reported to have had 'several Humming Birds and their Nests' in his grotto. An 1887 first edition of John Gould's lavishly illustrated six-volume monograph on the hummingbird family now retails at about £160,000. Gould painted the birds that he had acquired as skins for his own collection, which he exhibited to great approval at the Great Exhibition of 1851. He didn't see his first living hummer until 1857; all his work until then had been on the tiny smudges of still feathers.

Kingfisher

The Kingfisher – W. H. Davies
Kingfisher – Peter Scupham

'As kingfishers catch fire,' wrote Gerard Manley Hopkins, capturing the blue flame blaze of the birds in their rapid and direct flight. Kingfishers were believed to lay their eggs and raise their young on the surface of the sea, and if hung by the bill were thought to indicate, like natural weathercocks, the wind's direction. Sir Thomas Browne – Norfolk physician, philosopher, ostrich keeper, and responsible for the first record of a gannet for his county – doubted this. He suspected the myth of the halcyon was infecting the truth of the bird but wanted to make sure. He hung two kingfishers up 'with an untwisted silk in an open room'. They did not 'regularly conform their breasts' but pointed often 'to the opposite points of heaven'. In 2000 there was a maximum of 8,000 pairs of kingfishers in Britain. Its population across Europe is suffering because of pollution and river engineering schemes and is regarded as 'of conservation concern'. But it seems the British population is actually higher than it was. Some Victorian anglers, scared that the birds were better at fishing, ruthlessly persecuted the birds (special kingfisher traps were marketed); other fly-fishermen, in a hangover of some strain of sympathetic magic (see the grey heron and its feet), caught them to make flies from their feathers; taxidermists and collectors were drawn to their jewelled metallic shimmer.

Green Woodpecker

The Green Woodpecker's Nest – John Clare

Bright green, with a yellow rump and a red head, the green woodpecker manages to look both exotic and anciently part of the British scene. Feeding mostly on the ground, it eats ants, gathering them with its wonderfully long tongue, stored, when not in use, curled within its skull. Its ground feeding probably drew the bird into associations with 'other bird diggers of creation myths. It later became the bird of the plough and of fertility.'

The green woodpecker's laughing call gives it its common name of yaffle and versions of this are much reproduced in many of the recorded local names for the bird: Laughing Bird (Shropshire), Laughing Betsy (Gloucestershire), Yaffler (Hereford), Wood Yaffle (Suffolk), Yaffingale (Wiltshire, Hampshire), Yappingale (Somerset), Hefful, Heffalk (Yorkshire), Hickle, Stock-Feckle (Herefordshire), Eccle (Oxfordshire), Jack Eikle (Worcestershire), Icwell (Northamptonshire), Eaqual, Ecall (Shropshire), Yuckel (Gloucestershire).

Skylark

The Lark Ascending – George Meredith
To a Skylark – Percy Bysshe Shelley
The Caged Skylark – Gerard Manley Hopkins
Returning, We Hear the Larks – Isaac Rosenberg
Skylarks – Ted Hughes
The Skylark – John Clare
Shelley's Skylark – Thomas Hardy

Though nowadays the blackbird and perhaps the swallow rival it for pole position, the skylark remains, after the nightingale, the bird most often put into English poetry. In the late 1970s the British population of skylarks foundered and since then the bird has become increasingly scarce. It has appeared less in poetry too. Its fortunes are tied to farming – before open fields became widespread in Britain there were many skylarks, now what is being done to those open acres has led to the loss of at least a third of all skylarks. It is listed as a 'red species' of conservation concern and organizations like the RSPB are shifting some of their attention away from their previous flagship birds like avocets to devising plans (and buying farms) to save the skylark. The bird's song can still be heard widely, however, and it remains one of the most exhilarating of natural musics.

Woodlark

The Woodlark – Gerard Manley Hopkins

The woodlark is much less familiar than the skylark in Britain though it is arguably as good a singer. Though the total British population is much smaller than that of the troubled skylark, the woodlark has done well in recent years, benefiting from the increase in new-planted conifers and restored heathland. They are commoner now than they would have been in Hopkins's day. They sing in the same way – a beautiful thread of whistled sad notes that falls in pitch but increases in loudness.

Swallow

Anacreon's Ode to the Swallow – Elizabeth Barrett Browning
Itylus – Algernon Charles Swinburne
A Swallow – Ted Hughes
Augury – Caitríona O'Reilly
Swallows – Kathleen Jamie
The Swallows' Nest – Kathleen Jamie
The Swallow – Abraham Cowley

The swallow was the key bird as the mysteries of migration were untangled through centuries of interrogation. Its habit of feeding over water and roosting in reed beds didn't help human understanding, sustaining the belief that the birds hibernated at the bottom of ponds or in wet mud. Swallows were caught and kept through the winter in greenhouses with water butts. Though they showed no interest in diving below the surface, the hibernation theory was hard to dislodge; even Gilbert White, keenest of field observers, couldn't quite let it go. The swallow remains one of the most studied birds of present times. Experiments have been done stitching their beaks shut to see how far they can fly without feeding (not very, is the unsurprising answer); other researchers have snipped the birds' long outer tail feathers to assess their manoeuvrability and the tail's role in mate selection (males with super long tails are actually aerodynamically disabled but long tails are so appealing to females they are still worth having). Swallows have also been studied at Chernobyl, adjacent to the ruined nuclear reactor, where bent tail feathers and deformed beaks have been found along with other elevated levels of abnormalities in the birds innocently returning every spring to the radiation-contaminated fields of Byelorussia.

Tree Swallow

Feathering – Galway Kinnell

An American bird, the tree swallow is superficially similar to the European house martin. It is a stocky and broad-winged swallow found in the summer all the way north to Alaska. They are pale grey beneath and darker above; adult males have blue-green backs. It nests in holes in trees, on cliffs and commonly in specially erected bird boxes. 'Swallow' is thought to derive from an early Germanic word meaning 'cleft stick' that alludes to the forked tail of the birds.

Wagtail

Wagtail and Baby – Thomas Hardy

Hardy doesn't specify his species, but the pied wagtail, which often feeds around cattle, seems the most likely of the three wagtails that breed in Britain (pied, grey and yellow). Coleridge records a parallel observation to Hardy's poem in his notebook: 'Water Wagtails [he means pied], 7 or 8 following the feeding Horse in the pasture fluttering about & hopping close by his hoofs, under his belly and even so as often to tickle his nostrils with their pert Tail. The Horse shortens the grass & they get the insects.' In a letter (30 April 1915) to Lady Ottoline Morrell, D. H. Lawrence signed off with this observation: 'There is a wagtail sitting on the gate-post. I see how sweet and swift heaven is. But hell is slow and creeping and viscous and insect-teeming: as is this Europe now, this England. – *Vale!*'

Dipper

The Dipper – Kathleen Jamie

Dippers live on fast-running shallow rivers in upland areas. They are dumpy brown birds, like overgrown wrens, with a white throat and breast. They perch on boulders midstream, often with the water rushing over their feet. After scrutinizing the flow they walk into the river. And so they catch their insect food, walking on the streambed, often with its water fully over their heads. They reappear, breaking out of the river as if hatching from it, and return to their rock. A glaucous white eyelid wipes their dark eyes and they resume their watching.

Wren

The Cock's Nest – Norman Nicholson
Wren – Ted Hughes
Taxonomy – Helen Macdonald

Male wrens build nests as part of their courtship strategy and show prospective females around them like excited estate agents. Their nests are beautifully constructed domed affairs often stitched with inexplicable genius to their surroundings. They also nest in bizarre places: the desiccated carcass of a cat, a human skull, the pocket of a scarecrow's coat, a tramp's shirt left on a hedge, a pair of trousers hung up to dry, a nest within a magpie's nest – all these and many other sites have been reported.

The wren is not the smallest British bird – that is a goldcrest – but its size and its vigour relative to its size (its assertive cocked tail and extremely loud song for such a shrimp of a bird) may be behind the ancient European tradition that survived until the mid-twentieth century in Ireland and elsewhere, of New Year processions of people singing and chanting as they 'hunted' wrens, representing, so the great wren scholar and folklorist Edward Armstrong wrote, 'the defeat of the dark earth-powers and the identification with the hoped-for triumph of light and life'.

Northern Mockingbird

Bird-Witted – Marianne Moore
Patch Work – Thom Gunn

The mockingbird of American literature, including the two poems here as well as Walt Whitman's 'Out of the Cradle Endlessly Rocking' and Aretha Franklin's marvellous sung version of 1967, is a northern mockingbird. Mockingbirds are common in suburban USA; they are ten-inch-long grey and white birds, bold, aggressive even, and have an extraordinary song which seems to sample the neighbourhood – birds are mimicked and a host of other sounds processed into long musical songs of varied and repeated phrases. The species is widespread in southern North America and northern Mexico. In the last fifty years the bird has extended its breeding range northwards. Other mockingbirds are found in South America and the Caribbean.

Robin

from The White Devil – John Webster

The wren was once believed to be the robin's wife. There are many allusions in literature to the robin burying exposed dead or sleeping human bodies. The ballad of 'The Babes in the Wood' has the robin 'piously' covering the babes 'with leaves'. Izaak Walton describes the robin doing this as the bird 'that loves mankind both alive and dead'. A robin is described in Shakespeare's *Cymbeline* as a bird 'with charitable bill'. It is tempting to believe that these stories came from observation of real robins, who will pick through dead leaves seeking food, as well, as David Lack showed in his masterpiece monograph *The Life of the Robin*, as attending with vehemence to the stuffed bodies of rival robins should they be introduced into their territories. Lack writes: 'A popular Christmas card shows four or even more robins perching happily together on a holly branch. No more inappropriate symbol could be devised for the season of peace and goodwill. Should the incident occur in nature, furious conflicts would arise.'

Nightingale

Sonnet – John Milton
To the Nightingale – William Cowper
Ode to a Nightingale – John Keats
Early Nightingale – John Clare
The Nightingale's Nest – John Clare
The Nightingales – Ivor Gurney
'Herewith, a deep-delv'd draught' – Peter Reading

The nightingale is a small rufous brown thrush, not well marked but neat and straightforward in appearance. What comes out of its beak is another matter. The song is extraordinary though it is made more so by the conditions in which it is given and heard. In Europe and sometimes in Britain, nightingales commonly sing through the day and often perched in the open. Against the spring's generic musical fruit juice of warbler and thrush song, the nightingale's is striking – it is loud and sounds in pain, making musical lunges that seem to be cueing great stories – but it is not distinctive enough to earn the bird the standout top-song badge. But if sung at night, invisibly across darkened scrub and fields, towards an answering rival male half a mile away it takes on a different quality. Great jagged stabs of lyrical music are thrown into the summer night sky. The nightingale is increasingly rare in Britain – it has declined by 60 per cent since 1994.

Redstart

The Firetail's Nest – John Clare

The firetail is a local name for the redstart. The bird is small and robin-like but more richly marked. In summer males have a black face, a sooty grey back and brick red underparts. Both males and females have a warm rusty-red tail that quivers almost continuously regardless of what they are doing. Firetail describes it perfectly. Redstarts are migrant summer visitors to Britain and are most commonly found in upland oak woodlands. Aristotle believed they turned into robins in the winter because in Greece they disappeared about the time robins arrived.

Wheatear

The Wheat-Ear – Charlotte Smith

The wheatear is a summer visitor to Britain. It is a small thrush, a little larger than a robin, with a distinctive flashing square white rump. Its present name is derived from this feature, its 'white arse'. They breed in upland areas in holes in the ground (they like rabbit burrows) or in drystone walls, or scree, but they can be found almost anywhere on passage. They are hardy birds and are one of the first summer migrants to return to Britain each spring. Some of the same wheatears (ornithological nomenclature calls the species the northern wheatear, since there are many other wheatears in Europe and Africa) breed in northern Canada and Greenland and migrate to spend the winter south of the Sahara in west Africa, thereby undertaking one of the longest migrations of any land bird. To get from Greenland to southern Europe they make a thirty-hour non-stop flight.

Song Thrush

The Throstle – Alfred, Lord Tennyson
Evening Thrush – Ted Hughes

Mistle Thrush

The Darkling Thrush – Thomas Hardy
The Thrush – Edward Thomas

Thrush

The Thrush – Dafydd ap Gwilym (translated by Tony Conran)
Thrushes – Ted Hughes

The blackbird is also a thrush, but the song and mistle thrush are the two species we mean when we think of thrushes. Poets have confused the two as many people do. The song thrush is the smaller. It has warm brown upperparts, an ochre-washed black-speckled breast and it sings a warm song of repeated but musical notes. The blackbird's song is warmer still, but the mistle thrush's is decidedly cold. Its colouring – a grey tinged brown – and its rather stark face are also cool. It sings – often from the autumn onwards and often in wild and stormy weather from bare tree tops – throwing its cold and yelping song up into the sky. Tennyson's poem 'The Throstle' clearly describes a song thrush – its triple phrased song – and throstle (along with Mavis) is or was a widespread local name for the bird. Ted Hughes's 'Evening Thrush' also hurls three javelins of dew into the air, so is probably a song thrush. His poem 'Thrushes' about the birds on a lawn could refer to either species, as could Dafydd ap Gwilym's. Hardy's 'The Darkling Thrush' suggests a mistle thrush in its seasonal setting and the spartan song of the bird. Edward Thomas's 'The Thrush' does the same.

The song thrush is in trouble in Britain. On farmland the birds' numbers have fallen by 70 per cent because of a lack of food and shortage of nesting sites in the over tidied and industrialized countryside of southern Britain especially. These serious losses over the last forty years mean that a generation of children have grown up without necessarily knowing the bird's song as a backdrop to their lives.

Blackbird

'Sing a song of sixpence' – Anonymous
The Blackbird – William Barnes
Adlestrop – Edward Thomas
St Kevin and the Blackbird – Seamus Heaney

Though the nightingale has showbiz fame, the blackbird ought to be the best-loved songbird in Britain. It is generous in its song, it is offered in the most banal of places and is freely available through almost the entire country. And it is exquisite: musical, soft, fruited and balmy. It makes a soundtrack to spring and summer like no other bird.

In his autobiography, the pioneer bird song sound-recordist Ludwig Koch remembered how he was invited to meet Neville Chamberlain (then Chancellor of the Exchequer and 'a very keen bird-lover') after his recording of a blackbird song was broadcast on the BBC. He goes on:

After the Munich meeting a prominent Swiss paper attacked me for taking up the Prime Minister's time with listening to bird-song instead of to the voice of the threatened people of Czechoslovakia. The paper even claimed that Mr Chamberlain had left an important meeting in 1939 to listen to the unusual song of a blackbird in the garden of 10 Downing Street, who mimicked the repeated notes of a song-thrush.

Chiffchaff

The Pettichap's Nest – John Clare

The pettichap is an old and local name for a warbler. It is not totally certain which species is meant. The garden warbler is suggested by the *SOED*. But the chiffchaff has also been known as the lesser pettychap. John Clare's editors describe it as either a chiffchaff or a willow warbler. Both birds – closely related and not easy to separate in the field if they are not singing – build domed nests on or just above the ground in tangles of vegetation, as Clare's poem describes, but so does a garden warbler. Identification might be clinched by a prose note from elsewhere in Clare's papers, where he describes a little bird that has a note 'something like Pettichap whence his name'. Since the garden warbler and the willow warbler have elaborate songs and the chiffchaff says its name – *Zilpzalp*, it is called in German, for example – it seems most likely that the pettychap is a chiffchaff. Chiffchaffs, pale green above, colder grey below, are one of the first warblers to return to Britain in the spring. Gilbert White's journal entry for 3 April 1791 records hearing a chiffchaff, 'no bigger than a man's thumb, fetch an echo out of the hanger at every note'.

Long-tailed Tit

Bumbarrel's Nest – John Clare

The bumbarrel is a long-tailed tit. The local name (there are several variants known from across England) comes from the shape and construction of its domed nest, which is a remarkable and beautiful barrel-shaped felted assemblage of feathers (2,000 have been counted in one), moss, lichen, spider's silk and wool. Long-tailed tits might be a definition of sociability – they are never seen on their own and live through the year in quietly chatty gangs of birds, extended families that loop and *ping*, steered by their long tails into a bouncy progress, through woodland and scrub.

Chickadee

Flit – Mark Doty

The birds are not identified in Mark Doty's poem, but his lines suggest a winter feeding-party of chickadees. The black-capped is the most widespread across North America; it is black and white, and forms loose flocks in the winter that move together through woodland sharing lookouts for predators and capitalizing on food discoveries. Chickadees are the American equivalent of tits and behave in similar ways. Remarkable recent scientific studies have shown that black-capped chickadees are able to replace old neurons in their brains, which stored no-longer required information, with new neurons in order to remember, through the harshness of the North American winter, where they had cached seeds in the autumn in order to find them again. Alaskan chickadees – living in the harshest of winter environments – had better memories than birds living in the softer, easier south.

Shrike

The Shrike – Sylvia Plath

Sylvia Plath's poem is perhaps the most metaphorical of any of the poems here, but it is enriched by some knowledge of shrikes. They are hook-billed meat eaters and were known as 'butcher birds'. They were renowned for their larders – bushes where they impaled their prey (insects, mice, other birds) on thorns. Although they are passerines (perching birds), shrikes seem isolated among families of sweet singers and soft-billed birds. They are songbirds on their way to becoming raptors.

American Crow

To Victor Hugo of My Crow Pluto – Marianne Moore
Crows on the North Slope – W. S. Merwin
My Crow – Raymond Carver

Crows have crowded blackly into the human mind around the world. The American crow and the European crow are similar though separate species. Six species of crow (including two ravens) breed in North America. The poems here allude most probably to the American crow, *Corvus brachyrhynchos*, the commonest and most widespread corvid in America. Like all members of the crow family – ravens, jackdaws, magpies and jays – the crows are bundled with mythology and steeped in human-bird history. From the earliest stories about the creation of the world to present-day scientific research on avian intelligence, we and the crows have grown up together. Shifting some of the baggage has in itself become a poetic project, as the poems here show.

Carrion Crow

In Britain the carrion crow is one of the most widespread and successful of birds, probably because it can eat almost anything and live almost anywhere. They are the familiars of motorway verges and rubbish dumps and happy nesting on electricity pylons and tower blocks. They are not much loved and yet are perhaps – with ravens – the nearest we might get to a bird that is like us.

Rook

Carrion crows are seen in pairs or as single black birds picking their way through the modern world. Rooks are sociable and rural, like something out of the past. Their loose plumage around the base of their legs gives them baggy trousers; the adults' bare greyish-white chin and lores make their faces look older and somehow kinder than the carrion crow's uniform black severity. Pies can be made from slivers of young rook breast meat; some country pubs still serve them in the summer. Eating a carrion crow might seem, by comparison, like eating a rat.

Magpie

Like a male pheasant, if magpies weren't common their discovery would bring in hundreds of excited birders. They are striking birds, giving off a sense of great coherence, direction and bounce, their iridescent tail steering them, as T. H. White said, 'like a flying pan'. They are very common and successful in Britain but, though they happily gobble the eggs and chicks of other birds, several studies have shown that they have no overall adverse impact on songbird populations: 'Indeed in woodland songbird numbers were highest where magpie numbers were also at their highest.' Charles Causley would have known magpies from his native Cornwall. His poem describes a North American magpie; it is the same species.

Raven

from Noah's Ark – Anonymous
The Twa Corbies – Anonymous
The Ravens Nest – John Clare

The literature on the raven is vast; perhaps more has been written on the biggest of crows than on any other bird. In this it is helped by its worldwide distribution, its obviousness, and the long noticed and ancient connection between humans and the bird. The raven is the first bird mentioned in the Bible. In the Norse story of the beginning of the world, two ravens, Hugin and Munin, tell Odin what has been and what is to come. Ravens were observed around armies that gathered before battle and so appeared to be able to read the future. In fact, they were more simply remembering, as a species, the past. They knew blood and meat followed the clash of men. Banished by persecution through the nineteenth and twentieth centuries to remote and harsh uplands in Britain they are now returning to live among us, spreading back over the lowlands, darkening the sky over us once again. We may yet see them even more commonly. At the Roman town at Silchester in Hampshire raven bones are second in quantity only to chickens', suggesting ravens 'lived there in a semi-domestic state'.

Jackdaw

The Jack Daw – William Cowper

Jackdaws are the smallest members of the crow family in Britain. They live in permanent collectivity, breeding in scattered colonies, sometimes – catastrophically – in chimneys of village houses, feeding and flying together, and in almost continuous *chack*ing conversation. They have often been kept as pets. Their faces look intelligent. Their all-black bodies sootily focus to their dusty grey heads and their canny grey irises, the brightest of any British bird. Their eyes are morphologically analogous to human eyes, and a recent study found that captive jackdaws were sensitive to human expressions and were able to interpret them.

Blue Jay

The Blue Jay – D. H. Lawrence

The blue jay is widely distributed through the eastern half of North America. To a European's eyes – like D. H. Lawrence's – its blue seems electrically bright, as if fashioned from a metal not found in Europe. It is also noisy and conspicuous, even in towns and cities, and seems to come towards people as often as it flees from them. In this it seems very un-European. The jay in Britain has brilliant colours (including a tiny wing panel that looks loaned by the American blue jay) but is almost always seen hurrying away from any observer as if caught in flagrante up to no good.

Starling

Starlings Have Come – Ted Hughes
Mimics – David Hartnett
The Flock in the Firth – W. S. Herbert

On the Somerset Levels in recent winters up to 8 million starlings have gathered into vast pre-roost flocks. This is probably the largest gathering of birds ever seen in Britain. Starlings are, however, declining rapidly and are listed as a 'red' species, being of most concern. Urban and rural breeding populations are both down in numbers; the reasons for this are not fully understood. The starling has a long and varied literary life in Britain. John Clare called them Starnels, W. B. Yeats knew them as Stares, and Laurence Sterne drew attention to the proximity of his name to the bird in *A Sentimental Journey*. The birds themselves are fabulous mimics and expert world travellers. Introduced starlings have flourished in Fiji, Australia, New Zealand, the West Indies, South Africa, and above all in North America where, although behaving like European human settlers, they have been commonly despised. Starlings have crossed and colonized the entire American continent since arriving on the back of an eccentric plan by a drug-making millionaire to introduce to the USA all the birds mentioned in Shakespeare (Hotspur in *Henry IV, part 1*, plots to have a starling taught to say 'nothing but Mortimer' to 'gall and pinch this Bolingbroke'). In 1890–91 eighty pairs of European starlings were released in Central Park in New York City. Within eighty years it had become one of the most numerous birds in North America. Perhaps American starlings will one day come to the help of their European ancestors.

House Sparrow

The Dead Sparrow – William Cartwright
Mr and Mrs Spikky Sparrow – Edward Lear
House Sparrows – Michael Longley
For the House Sparrow, in Decline – Paul Farley
Sparrow – Andrew Motion

A decree in Dresden in 1559 commended 'the Christian zeal of the worthy and pious parson Daniel Greysser,' for having 'put under ban the sparrows, on account of their unceasing and extremely vexatious chatterings and scandalous unchastity during the sermon, to the hindrance of God's word and of Christian devotion'. In November 2005, a house sparrow was shot (to international outcry) in the Netherlands after it had got into a hall and knocked over 23,000 dominos that had been set up for a domino-toppling competition.

The poetic house sparrow has moved from the default quotidian dusty town bird, chirruping in the eaves, to the surprise rarity, the ubiquitous bird that has suddenly vanished. There are still between 6 and 7 million pairs in Britain but this is 10 million fewer birds than twenty-five years ago.

Bullfinch

On the Death of Mrs Throckmorton's Bulfinch (1788) –
    William Cowper

Bullfinches are among the quietest and most discreet birds of Britain. They seem shy and almost apologetic as they pick their way along hedgerows or through open woodland; their calls and song are likewise among the most modest of any bird. Their soft rosy pink plumage adds to their blush. Yet the bird is also a remarkable mimic – caged bullfinches have long been known for their ability to learn tunes whistled to them. In Thomas Hardy's *Tess of the d'Urbervilles*, Tess has to whistle for the pet bullfinches as part of her job at the house of Mrs d'Urberville. Until 1999 bullfinches could be trapped and killed in Britain in fruit growing areas, where they were regarded as pests in orchards. It has been proved such killing has no impact on the population, but overall numbers of the bird have plummeted in the last thirty years, probably because of the loss of feeding and nesting habitat throughout lowland Britain.

Goldfinch

The Caged Goldfinch – Thomas Hardy

Goldfinches were caged for their song – a lovely liquid metallic tinkle – and their red and gold flashes of plumage, and perhaps too because of their association with Christ. Because it eats thistle seeds the bird has been connected with Christ's crown of thorns and it appears in paintings of the Madonna and Child to represent the Crucifixion ahead.

On 11 September 1826, William Cobbett's rural ride took him to Wiltshire, where:

Between Somerford and Ocksey, I saw on the side of the road, more *goldfinches* than I had ever seen together; I think fifty times as many as I had ever seen at one time in my life. The favourite food of the goldfinch is the seed of the *thistle*. This seed is just now dead ripe. The thistles are all cut and carried away from the *fields* by the harvest; but, they grow alongside the roads; and in this place, in great quantities. So that the goldfinches were got here in flocks, and, as they continued to fly along before me, for nearly half a mile, and still sticking to the roads and the banks, I do believe I had, at last, a flock of ten thousand flying before me.

Greenfinch

The Green Linnet – William Wordsworth

Green linnet is an old name for the greenfinch. Slightly larger than a linnet and with a heavier bill, the greenfinch is richly painted: males are moss green with numerous splashes of bright yellow in their wings and tail. They have lovely warming songs of canary-like trills, whistles and twitters. They also have a more soporific wheezing note. In spring males perform song flights, where they fly with deep and slow wing beats (known as 'bat flight' though it doesn't actually seem bat-like at all), their body rolling from side to side, singing and calling all the time.

Siskin

Siskin – Anne Stevenson

The siskin seems a delicate and gentle bird. It is like a neighbour to the greenfinch, slighter, mostly quieter and less well marked. They breed in conifer woods and eat spruce and pine seeds. It has increased in numbers in Britain and has learned to use and love garden seed feeders.

Snow Bunting

Snow Bunting – Michael Longley

The snow bunting is mostly a winter visitor to Britain and Ireland, though a very few pairs breed on the high scree slopes of the Cairngorms in Scotland. The tinkling call described by Michael Longley is often what attracts a bird-watcher's attention to the bird. Though they are brightly marked, with black and white wings and tail and undersides and sandy heads and backs, and usually are seen in small flocks, they are remarkably well camouflaged on the beaches and coastal fields where they are most commonly seen in the winter. If snow lies they are almost invisible. These wintering birds coming from Iceland and Scandinavia look like arctic soldiers on exercises.

Yellowhammer

The Yellowhammer's Nest – John Clare
The Yellowhammer – John Clare

The male yellowhammer is the brightest yellow bird commonly seen in Britain. It has a yellow head and underparts and a chestnut rump and often perches on the tops of hedges and trees and sings. Its 'little bit of bread and no cheese' song is widely recognized. In 2000, 792,000 territories were recorded, but the bird has been described as being in 'dire straits'. Until the 1980s the population seemed stable but since then the yellowhammer has been lost as a breeding bird in many areas. Changes in farming methods and intensity (the increasing absence of uncultivated field edges and of winter stubble) seem to blame. The 'hammer' of the bird is thought to come from an Old English name 'amer' that, as *Ammer*, still means bunting today in German.

Ovenbird

The Oven Bird – Robert Frost

A beautiful small and intense North American warbler, the ovenbird looks like a cross between a pipit and a goldcrest. It forages on the ground in shaded woodland and gets its name from its nest, which is a dome of dead leaves with a side entrance, reminiscent of a 'Dutch' oven. It winters in South America and its passage down the Atlantic seaboard explains why there have been four records in Britain since the first in Shetland in 1973. These birds would have been involuntarily scooped up and blown across the ocean, to the delight of British bird-watchers. The individuals almost certainly died not long after making landfall or would have continued even further in the errant direction they had started on to get yet more lost, deeper into Europe.

Oriole

'To hear an Oriole sing' – Emily Dickinson
The Orioles – John Ashbery

Emily Dickinson's orioles are different from any oriole a British poet might write about (the golden oriole is an extremely rare breeder in Britain, though common in Europe). New World orioles – there are twenty-four species (seven are regular breeders in North America) – are members of the *Icteridae* family, which only occurs in the Americas. They were given the oriole name because of the similarity in appearance to the Eurasian golden oriole – they are gorgeous birds flaming with aureate colours. Two species, the Baltimore and the orchard oriole, occur in the Amherst district and Emily Dickinson and John Ashbery could have seen either, though the Baltimore is perhaps the stronger candidate.

Red-winged Blackbird

Thirteen Ways of Looking at a Blackbird – Wallace Stevens

Wallace Stevens's blackbird, like Emily Dickinson's oriole, is also not the same bird as the European bird of the same name. American blackbirds are not thrushes but Icterids, like the American orioles. The red-winged blackbird is the most widespread and the most likely species for Wallace Stevens's poem, though it must be said that the poem has an echo of the nursery rhyme 'Sing a Song of Sixpence' with its four and twenty blackbirds and also that Stevens was fond of putting birds in his poetry that resist specific identification. What is the bird with coppery, keen claws, for example? It is called a parakeet, but we struggle to clinch any identification. Not that this matters, but it should caution us in tying red-winged blackbirds too seriously to his blackbird poem.

Sources and Further Reading

Recent population figures are mostly taken from the websites of the BTO and the RSPB. North American species are well covered by the Cornell Laboratory of Ornithology website. *Birds in England* by Andy Brown and Phil Grice (2005) is excellent for more detailed information.

For identification: *Collins Bird Guide* by Lars Svensson and Peter J. Grant (1999) is the key European book, the *Sibley Guide to Birds* by David Allen Sibley (2000) the same for North America.

For in-depth ornithology: Stanley Cramp et al., eds., *Handbook of the Birds of Europe, the Middle East, and North Africa: The Birds of the Western Palearctic* (1977–94), and J. del Hoyo, A. Elliott and J. Sargatal, eds., *Handbook of the Birds of the World* (1992–continuing).

For biology: Frank B. Gill, *Ornithology* (2007).

For birds and human culture: *Birds Britannica* by Mark Cocker and Richard Mabey (2005). Older books of great value include: J. H. Gurney, *Early Annals of Ornithology* (1921), C. E. Hare, *Bird Lore* (1952), Edward A. Armstrong, *The Folklore of Birds* (1958), James Fisher, *The Shell Bird Book* (1966), Francesca Greenoak, *All the Birds of the Air: The Names, Lore and Literature of British Birds* (1981). Peggy Munsterberg, *The Penguin Book of Bird Poetry* (1984) is a remarkable compendium of earlier centuries of bird poems.

Also recommended: Michael Walters, *A Concise History of Ornithology* (2005), Peter Bircham, *A History of Ornithology* (2007), Christopher W. Leahy, *The Birdwatcher's Companion to North American Birdlife* (2006), and Tim Birkhead, *The Wisdom of Birds* (2008).

For esoterica: *Winged Wonders*, ed. Peter Watkins and Jonathan Stockland (2005), William Yarrell, *A History of British Birds*, 4th edn, rev. Alfred Newton and Howard Saunders (1871–4), *The Chatto Book of Cabbages and Kings*, ed. Francis Spufford (1989), *The Oxford Book of Creatures*, ed. Fleur Adcock and Jacqueline Sims (1995).

Cited references

Ostrich: Sir Thomas Browne, *Selected Writings*, ed. Claire Preston (1995), p. 131.

Ostrich: Samuel Taylor Coleridge, *Biographia Literaria* (1952), p. 24.

Ostrich: William Wordsworth, from *The Prelude* (1805), book 3, lines 307–9, *The Prelude 1799, 1805, 1850*, ed. Jonathan Wordsworth, M. H. Abrams and Stephen Gill (1979), p. 106.

Gannet: J. H. Gurney, *Early Annals of Ornithology* (1921), pp. 95, 195–6.

Cormorant: Samuel Taylor Coleridge, *Selected Letters*, ed. H. J. Jackson (1988), p. 31.

Cormorant: John Milton, *Paradise Lost*, book 4, lines 196–7.

Goose: Samuel Taylor Coleridge, *Notebooks, A Selection*, ed. Seamus Perry (2002), p. 31.

Goose: Pliny the Elder, *Natural History, A Selection*, trans. John F. Healy (2004), p. 144.

Goose: E. P. Evans, *The Criminal Prosecution and Capital Punishment of Animals* (first published 1906, reissued 1987), p. 177.

Red Kite: J. H. Gurney, *Early Annals of Ornithology* (1921), p. 82.

Kestrel: Thomas Nashe, *Lenten Stuff* (1599).

Turkey: Christopher W. Leahy, *The Birdwatcher's Companion to North American Birdlife* (2004), p. 842.

Turkey: Michael Walters, *A Concise History of Ornithology* (2003), p. 31.

Cock and Hen: Henry Tristram, *The Natural History of the Bible* (1868).

Pheasant: Mark Cocker and Richard Mabey, *Birds Britannica* (2005), p. 169.

Dodo: Oliver Goldsmith quoted in Fleur Adcock and Jacqueline Simms, *The Oxford Book of Creatures* (1995), p. 359.

Dodo: Lewis Carroll, *Alice's Adventures in Wonderland* (1998), p. 26.

Rock Dove/Feral Pigeon: Graham Robb, *Rimbaud* (2000), pp. 258–9.

Wood Pigeon: Samuel Taylor Coleridge, *Poet to Poet*, ed. James Fenton (2006).

Parakeet: Andy Brown and Phil Grice, *Birds in England* (2005), p. 421.

Cuckoo: Michael Walters, *A Concise History of Ornithology* (2003), p. 167.

Tawny Owl: Gilbert White, *The Natural History of Selborne*, ed. James Fisher (1960), p. 127.

Barn Owl: Beatrix Potter quoted in Fleur Adcock and Jacqueline Simms, *The Oxford Book of Creatures* (1995), p. 40.

Nightjar: Gilbert White, *Journals*, ed. Walter Johnson (1971), p. 341.

Whippoorwill: Henry Thoreau, in *The Bird-Lover's Bedside Book*, ed. R. M. Lockley (1960), p. 65.

Swift: Gilbert White, *Journals*, ed. Walter Johnson (1971), p. 260.

Hummingbird: Francis Spufford, *The Chatto Book of Cabbages and Kings* (1989), p. 123.

Kingfisher: Sir Thomas Browne, *Selected Writings*, ed. Claire Preston (1995), p. 121.

Green Woodpecker: Francesca Greenoak, *All the Birds of the Air – The Names, Lore and Literature of British Birds* (1981), p. 183.

Wagtail: Samuel Taylor Coleridge, *Notebooks, A Selection*, ed. Seamus Perry (2002), p. 97.

Wagtail: D. H. Lawrence, *Collected Letters*, ed. Harry T. Moore (1977) vol. 2, p. 338.

Wren: Edward A. Armstrong, *The Folklore of Birds* (1959), p. 166.

Robin: C. E. Hare, *Bird Lore* (1952), p. 29.

Robin: David Lack, *The Life of the Robin* (1943), p. 51.

Blackbird: Ludwig Koch, *Memoirs of a Birdman* (1955), p. 41.

Chiffchaff: Eric Robinson and Richard Fitter, *John Clare's Birds* (1982), p. 50.

Chiffchaff: Gilbert White, *Journals*, ed. Walter Johnson (1971), p. 380.

Magpie: T. H. White, quoted in Fleur Adcock and Jacqueline Simms, *The Oxford Book of Creatures* (1995), p. 38.

Magpie: Andy Brown and Phil Grice, *Birds in England* (2005), p. 560.

Raven: J. H. Gurney, *Early Annals of Ornithology* (1921), p. 16.

Jackdaw: *Current Biology* 19, 14 April 2009, pp. 602–6.

House Sparrow: E. P. Evans, *The Criminal Prosecution and Capital Punishment of Animals* (first published 1906, reissued 1987), pp. 127–8.

Goldfinch: William Cobbett, *Rural Rides*, ed. George Woodcock (1830 edition, reissued 1967), p. 367.

Tim Dee

Poem Acknowledgements

Adcock, Fleur: 'The Last Moa' from *Poems 1960–2000* (2005), reproduced by permission of Bloodaxe Books; Ashbery, John: 'The Orioles' from *Selected Poems*, reproduced by permission of Carcanet Press; Auden, W. H.: 'Short Ode to the Cuckoo' from *Collected Poems*, reproduced by permission of Faber and Faber Ltd; Barker, George: 'On a Bird Dead in the Road' from *Street Ballads*, reproduced by permission of Faber and Faber Ltd; Causley, Charles: 'Magpie' from *Collected Poems 1951–1997*, published by Macmillan, reproduced by permission of David Higham Associates Ltd; Clarke, Gillian: 'Curlew' and 'Neighbours' from *Collected Poems,* reproduced by permission of Carcanet Press; Cook, Stanley: 'Bird-nesting' reproduced by permission of The Poetry Business Ltd; Douglas, Keith: 'The Sea Bird' from *The Complete Poems,* reproduced by permission of Faber and Faber Ltd; Dunmore, Helen: 'Heron' from *Out of the Blue: Poems 1975–2000* (2001), reproduced by permission of Bloodaxe Books; Farley, Paul: 'For the House Sparrow, in Decline' from *The Ice Age* (2002) and 'The Heron' from *Tramp in Flames* (2006), both reproduced by permission of Pan Macmillan, London © Paul Farley; Feaver, Vicki: 'Wood-Pigeons' from *The Handless Maiden* by Vicki Feaver, published by Jonathan Cape. Reprinted by permission of The Random House Group Ltd; Fenton, James: 'The Orange Dove of Fiji' (© James Fenton), reproduced by permission of PFD (www.pfd.co.uk) on behalf of James Fenton; Ford, Mark: 'Passenger Pidgeon', reproduced by kind permission of the poet; Frost, Robert: 'The Exposed Nest', 'On a Bird Singing in its Sleep' and 'The Oven Bird' from *The Poetry of Robert Frost*, edited by Edward Connery Lathem, published by Jonathan Cape. Reprinted by

Anne: 'Siskin' from *The Collected Poems: 1955–2005* (2005), reproduced by permission of Bloodaxe Books; Tate, James: 'The Blue Booby' from *Selected Poems*, reproduced by permission of Carcanet Press; Thomas, Dylan: 'Over Sir John's Hill' from *The Poems*, published by Dent. Reproduced by permission of David Higham Associates Ltd; Tomlinson, Charles: 'To be Engraved on the Skull of a Cormorant' from *Selected Poems 1955*, reproduced by permission of Carcanet Press; Wright, Kit: 'The Sub-Song', reproduced by kind permission of the poet; Yeats, W. B.: 'Leda and the Swan. Reproduced by permission of A. P. Watt Ltd on behalf of Gráinne Yeats.

Index of First Lines

I found a pigeon's skull on the machair, 249
If, tonight, she scorns me for my song, 10
I had a dove and the sweet dove died, 97
I leant upon a coppice gate When Frost was spectre-gray, 202
In a deep, in a dark wood, somewhere north of Loch Lomond, 69
Incorrigible, unmusical, 77
In past centuries it was believed that migrating birds would winter on the moon
   276
In this one of all fields I know the best 77
I sit in the top of the wood, my eyes closed. 49
I stood on a dark summit, among dark summits – 64
is what they called it, shaking their heads 276
It had been badly shot. 36
I thought it a piece of fancifulness 176
I thought I was so tough, 50
It is an ancient Mariner, 6
It's evening on the river, 29
Its name describes it, even to those penholder patches 47
It was the Rainbow gave thee birth, 135
It was winter, near freezing, 168
I wish my whole battened heart were a property 162

Just by the wooden brig a bird flew up 266

Lauda, anima mea, Dominum! 14
Lover of swamps 88

Magnetic winds from the sun pour in 161
Men heard this roar of parleying starlings, saw, 132
Mostly it is a pale face hovering in the afterdraught 122
Music of a thrush, clearbright 205
My heart aches, and a drowsy numbness pains My sense, 188

No longer country clubber, 256
No one now imagines you answer idle questions 120
Now westlin winds, and slaught'ring guns 81

O blithe new-comer! I have heard, 118
Of: my crow Pluto, 225

Often, for pastime, mariners will ensnare 5
Old Adam, the carrion crow, 229
Older than the ancient Greeks, than 97
oldest known feathered fossil evidence, 41
On a little piece of wood, Mr Spikky Sparrow stood; 252
One of the most begrudging avian take-offs 29
O nightingale, that on yon bloomy spray Warbl'st at eve, 186
On our side of the glass You laid out the blackbird's 250
On shallow slates the pigeons shift together, 100
On Sunday the hawk fell on Bigging 48
On the day of the explosion 214
On the slopes of Taveuni 104
On the stiff twig up there Hunches a wet black rook 233
O the cuckoo she's a pretty bird, 118
Out of the wood of thoughts that grows by night 63
Ov all the birds upon the wing 208
Over Sir John's hill, 55

Repeat that, repeat, 120
Rooks flew across the sky, bright February watched 233

She dips her bill in the rim of the sea. 86
She dotes on what the wild birds say 184
Shutters, broken, firewood, a rake, 163
Sing a song of sixpence a pocket full of rye, 208
Skeins o geese write a word 35
Skirting the river road, (my forenoon walk, my rest,) 44
Small bird with green plumage, 264
Sombre the night is, 147
Something to do with territory makes them sing, 182
Somewhere afield here something lies 153
Somewhere in the bush, the last moa 42
So zestfully canst thou sing? 80
Sumer is icumen in, Loud sing cuckoo! 117
'Summer is coming, summer is coming. 199
Swallow, my sister, O sister swallow, 158
Sweet Suffolk owl, so trimly dight 121

Yesterday she took down from the attic 165
Your numbers fall and it's tempting to think 256
You ruffled black blossom, 59
You said you would kill it this morning. 71
You suit me well; for you can make me laugh, 64
You were forever finding some new play. 215

Index of Poets

Selected Poems

ROGER MCGOUGH

Selected Poems consists of work chosen by the poet himself from *Collected Poems*, published by Penguin in 2004, together with several new, previously unpublished poems. The complete span of McGough's writing, from the 1960s to the new millennium, is represented.

'McGough is a true original and more than one generation would be much the poorer without him' *The Times*

'Memorable and enduring and fresh. Age has not withered [his lines] nor diminished his potency. Of how much modern poetry can you say that?' *Sunday Herald*

'Over forty years ago, this shy Liverpudlian asked Poetry if it was dancing. Since then we have all, readers and poets alike, come out of the hushed libraries and the solemn universities to join in the party. We are lucky indeed to have him' Carol Ann Duffy

'McGough has done for British poetry what champagne does for weddings' *Time Out*

'No detail of daily life, trivial, ridiculous or touching, is unworthy of sympathetic attention … honest, enlivening' Alan Brownjohn, *Sunday Times*

SELECTED POEMS

SOPHIE HANNAH

Since her first book was published in 1995, Sophie Hannah has been recognized as one of the best young poets on the scene. Chosen by *The Times* in 1999 as the 'New Writer to Watch' and in the same year by the Daily Telegraph as one of the 'Stars of the New Millennium', she has published four bestselling collections. This is the first selection of her poems to appear in one volume.

'Sophie Hannah is among the best at comprehending in rhyming verse the indignity of having a body and the nobility of having a heart' *Guardian*

'Shall I put it in capitals? SOPHIE HANNAH IS A GENIUS' *Poetry Review*

'The brightest young star in British poetry' *Independent*

'A wonderful poet' *Observer*

'Her rhyming is as convoluted and densely patterned as her subjects are intractable. Hannah answers the tangled miseries of everyday life with complex internal argument and layering of sounds, and moves through minefields of emotion with instinctive grace' *The Times Educational Supplement*

'Her range is astonishing: most readers will come away having been changed or delighted' *Daily Telegraph*

'A poet of considerable skill . . . A shrewd and accurate observer of the world around her, and of her own life, she is often very funny' *Oldie*

SELECTED POEMS

GEOFFREY HILL

This first selection of Geoffrey Hill's poetry charts the evolution of a complex, uncompromising, visionary body of work over fifty years. It includes poems from Hill's astonishing debut, *For the Unfallen*, through the verset-sequence *Mercian Hymns*, to acclaimed recent work, including *The Orchards of Syon* and *Without Title*.

Praise for Geoffrey Hill:

'Critics queue up to say, unequivocally, that he is the best poet working in English' Tom Payne, *Daily Telegraph*

'One of the big, mind-altering talents at work in any medium' Grey Gowrie, *Spectator*

'The finest British poet of our time' John Hollander

'Hill is the greatest living poet in the English language' Nicholas Lezard

'It is impossible in a short space to convey not merely how good, but how important Geoffrey Hill's writing is . . . There is no one alive writing in our language about deeper or more important matters, no one saying such interesting things . . . The work of Hill is a phoenix rising from European ashes' A. N. Wilson, *Spectator*

'Whatever the densities of Hill's expression, or the powerful impacted forces in his syntax and rhythms, this poetry achieves a strength, memorability and precision beyond the abilities of any poet writing in English' Peter McDonald, *The Times Literary Supplement*

He just wanted a decent book to read ...

Not too much to ask, is it? It was in 1935 when Allen Lane, Managing Director of Bodley Head Publishers, stood on a platform at Exeter railway station looking for something good to read on his journey back to London. His choice was limited to popular magazines and poor-quality paperbacks – the same choice faced every day by the vast majority of readers, few of whom could afford hardbacks. Lane's disappointment and subsequent anger at the range of books generally available led him to found a company – and change the world.

'We believed in the existence in this country of a vast reading public for intelligent books at a low price, and staked everything on it'
Sir Allen Lane, 1902–1970, founder of Penguin Books

The quality paperback had arrived – and not just in bookshops. Lane was adamant that his Penguins should appear in chain stores and tobacconists, and should cost no more than a packet of cigarettes.

Reading habits (and cigarette prices) have changed since 1935, but Penguin still believes in publishing the best books for everybody to enjoy. We still believe that good design costs no more than bad design, and we still believe that quality books published passionately and responsibly make the world a better place.

So wherever you see the little bird – whether it's on a piece of prize-winning literary fiction or a celebrity autobiography, political tour de force or historical masterpiece, a serial-killer thriller, reference book, world classic or a piece of pure escapism – you can bet that it represents the very best that the genre has to offer.

Whatever you like to read – trust Penguin.